JAPAN IN YOUR POCKET

JAPAN IN YOUR POCKET

A STEP-BY-STEP GUIDE
AND TRAVEL ITINERARY

BY DAVID OLD

Horizon Books

British Library Cataloguing in Publication Data

Old, David
  Japan in your pocket: a step-by-step guide
  and travel itinerary. (Pocket travellers)
  1. Japan. Visitors' guides
  I. Title II. Series
  915.2'0448

  ISBN 1-85461-020-1

© 1987 by David Old
UK edition © 1989 by Horizon Books Ltd

Maps Deborah Reade

All rights reserved. No part of this work may be reproduced, other than for the purposes of review, or stored in an information retrieval system, without the express permission of the Publishers given in writing.

This edition first published in 1989 by Horizon Books Ltd, Harper & Row House, Estover Road, Plymouth PL6 7PZ, United Kingdom. Tel: Plymouth (0752) 705251. Telex: 45635. Fax: (0752) 777603.

Printed in Great Britain by BPCC Wheatons Ltd, Exeter

CONTENTS

How to Use This Book	8
Basic Travel Hints	14
Itinerary	23
Tour 1 Helpful Hints	26
Arrive in Tokyo	26
Tour 2 Explore Tokyo	33
Tour 3 More of Tokyo	36
Tour 4 Izu Peninsula – Shimoda – Toi	40
Tour 5 Toi and Matsuzaki	44
Tour 6 Ise	45
Tour 7 Ise – Kyoto	48
Tour 8 Kyoto	52
Tour 9 Kyoto – Nara	57
Tour 10 Himeji and Kotohira	60
Tour 11 Miyajima	64
Tour 12 Miyajima	67
Tour 13 Hiroshima – Travel to Kyushu	68
Tour 14 Yobuko Town – Hatomizaki	73
Tour 15 Hatomizaki – Kyoto	76
Tour 16 Travel to Hakui	77
Tour 17 Travel to Sado Island	79
Tour 18 Sado	81
Tour 19 Sado to Bandai	84
Tour 20 Travel to Nikko	87
Tour 21 Chuzenji/Nikko	90
Tour 22 Nikko-Tokyo	92
Post Tour Option: Hokkaido	94
Brief History of Japan	105
Language	110
Japanese Food	119
More Useful Information	124
Festivals	124
Information Sources	126
Youth Hostels	127

Japan in Your Pocket

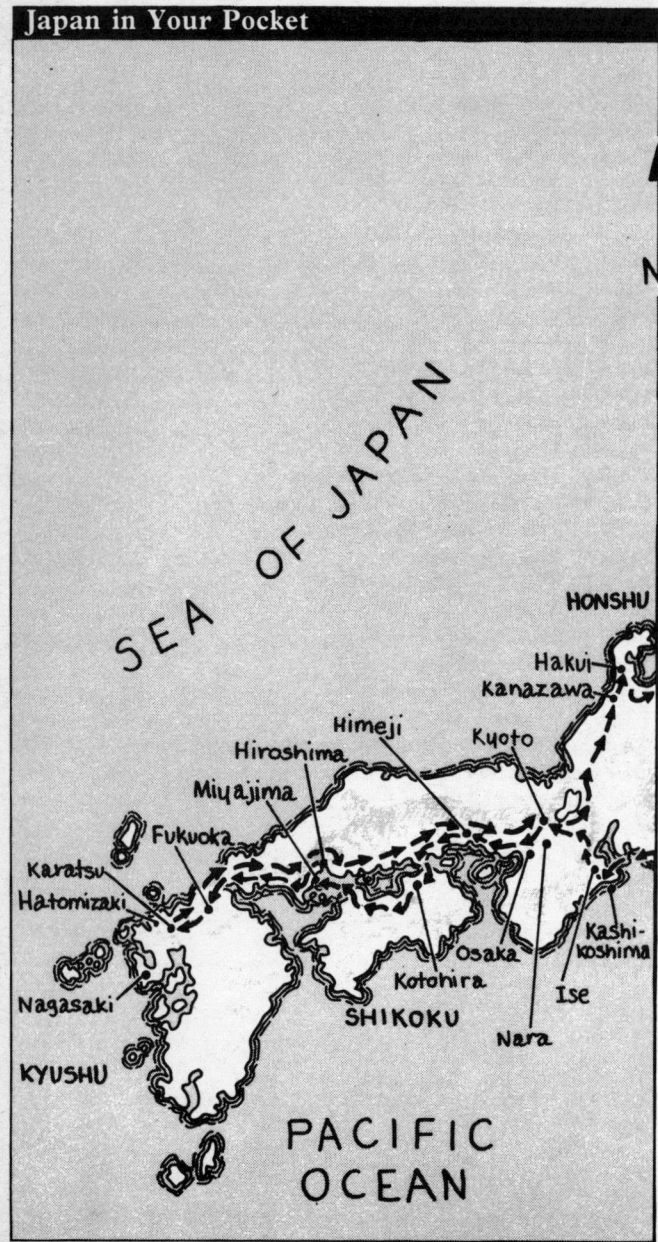

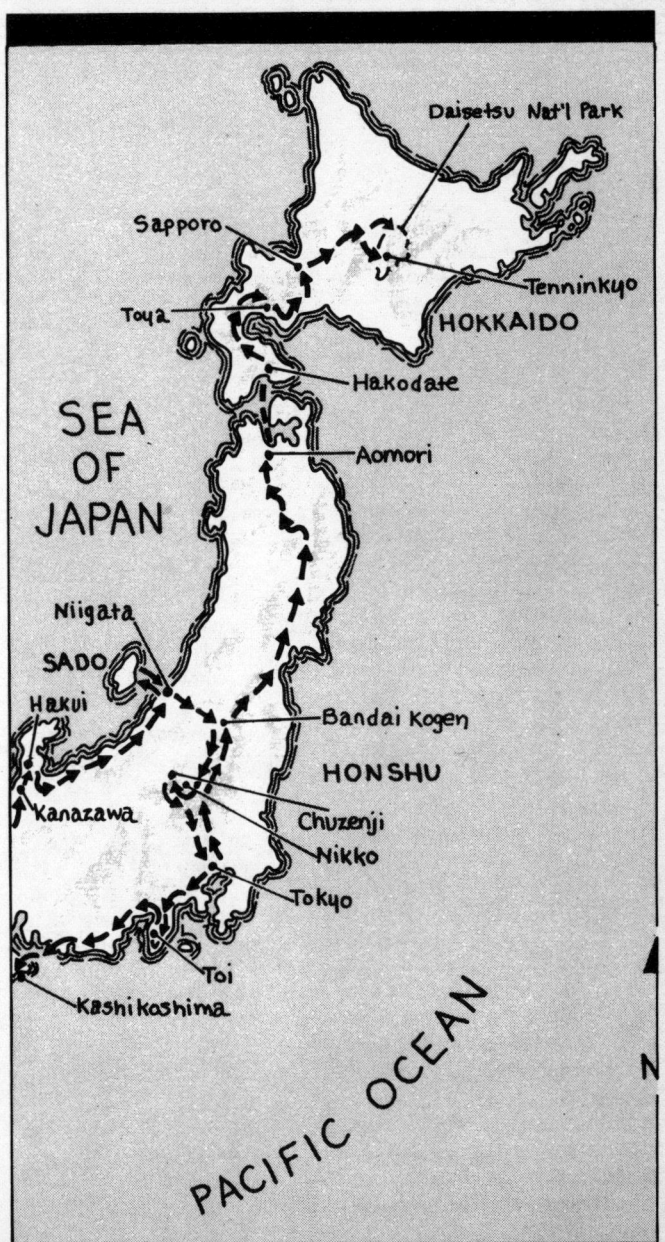

HOW TO USE THIS BOOK

This book is the tour guide in your pocket, a tried and proven plan to see Japan in a few short weeks. It gives you the travel efficiency of an organised tour plus do-it-yourself freedom and flexibility.

Japan in Your Pocket tells you how to get the most out of Japan's super-modern Bullet Trains using a rail pass that's only available to foreigners (that's us). Ferries, local trains and buses will take you deep into the countryside where tourists are rare and the English language might as well be double dutch. You'll eat and sleep Japanese-style in traditional country inns known as minshuku and ryokan.

This book is a selective, not comprehensive, travel guide. The Japanese like to group their sightseeing highlights by threes: 'One of the nation's three most beautiful gardens' (or islands, or waterfalls). In this itinerary I won't take you to all three gardens, only the best of the three. Which one is 'best', of course, is my personal opinion — based on fifteen trips to Japan, a total of over twenty-four months travelling, studying and living there. Besides Japan's 'bests' and 'most beautifuls', I'll show you some totally unique places that other guidebooks never mention — including my favourite picnic spot.

Efficient travellers think ahead. Read the whole book as you plan the trip. Modify the plan to suit your schedule and interests. If you want to see a place that's not in the itinerary, rearrange the itinerary. My tours connect destinations by the easiest routes, so if you want to break off, wait until you get in the general neighbourhood.

Once you've started the trip, it may be difficult to alter your plans without missing accommodation you've reserved and perhaps prepaid. Lodging reservations are much more important in Japan (especially away from big cities) than in most western nations. Even the youth hostel style National Citizens' Hotels are often booked up months in advance.

The itinerary format I've used in this book is divided into 22 tours, containing:

1. A **general overview** for the tour.
2. A **suggested schedule** for the tour.
3. A list of major **sightseeing highlights.** These are rated in order of importance: ●●● Don't miss; ●● Try hard to see; and ● See if you get a chance.
4. **Transport** — trains, buses and ferries, how to find them and when to go.

How to Use This Book

5. **Food and accommodation** — where to find the best of each.

6. **Helpful hints,** random titbits of information that will help your day go better.

7. Clear, user-friendly **maps**. To get the most out of them, learn the following symbols:

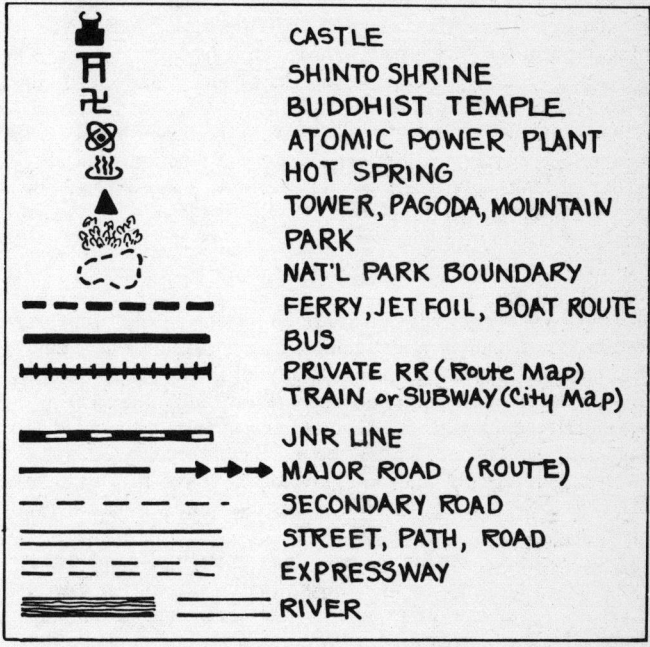

At the back of the book you will find information covering language, food, history and festivals. Read these last pages along with the first. A Hokkaido **post-tour option** is there for people who just can't get enough.

Nobody does it better

In *Japan in Your Pocket* I present what I personally consider to be an ideal plan for touring Japan — but let's face it, I'm not you. Read every piece of information you can lay your hands on ahead of time, customise this itinerary and design your own perfect trip. A self-guided tour has many advantages, but it also means you do the work of the tour company, making advance arrangements which, in Japan, are especially important. The Japanese national character is fanatically organised, so touring the country requires more organisation than other parts of the world.

Very few Japanese travel without reservations, so innkeepers expect them. You can turn up out of the blue and still find a place to stay if necessary, but the more reservations you have and can stick to, the easier your trip will be. You can travel at will, unhindered, but most people do better sticking to a schedule for comfort's sake. By reserving ahead you will also save your Japanese hosts a lot of anxiety by informing them that they should expect a Gaijin (foreigner) under their roof. Remember that once off the beaten path, non-Japanese faces can be rare. The more you plan and organise ahead, the smoother, easier and more enjoyable your tour will be.

Lay out your own travel plan following the book itinerary when convenient. If you would rather see more of Kyoto instead of going on to an out-of-the-way (and beautiful) island or castle, by all means join up with the book a day or two later. Just plan ahead to avoid confusion.

When to go

Japan covers many lines of latitude, so picking an ideal time to go can be tough. Unless you're going skiing, Hokkaido would be a bad choice in the winter, just as nearly all the rest of the country is very hot from late June to August. Fortunately, the locals take their main national holiday from the end of July to the middle of August. I say "main" holiday because they take many other vacations throughout the year. For example if you plan to be in the Inland Sea during cherry blossom time, you will absolutely need reservations.

Spring and autumn are the best times to travel, but other times have their advantages as well. Tokyo can be gorgeous at dawn in December. The warmth of Kyushu's beaches is only a morning's train ride from a frigid, foggy Kyoto morning. If you could only go in winter you could focus more on the hot springs which abound all over the country. You would see Mt Fuji at its finest: snow-capped. The island of Sado would be a definite miss unless you have a passion for violent sea storms. (They're astonishing!) On the other hand, you could live in the beautiful clear waters around Sado in July or August.

Spring and autumn are best; any other time of year runs a close second.

Cost

Yes, the land of the rising yen is expensive. The cost of rooms and transport is as high as almost anywhere else in the world. But you'll feel you've got more than your money's worth when you return home. You'll have far more than just photos and souvenirs to show for your trip: you will have experienced one of the world's most unique and influential cultures.

About £1,750 apiece will do the trick for airfare, rail pass, accommodation and meals. This figure doesn't allow a lot to play with, but you'll be staying in quality ryokan and minshuku. You could economise if necessary by staying in youth hostels where available (see the listing in the back of the book), avoiding car rentals and taxis, and cutting corners on lunches and nightlife. However, if you go for broke the richness of the experience will be worth a lot more than the dent in your wallet, I promise.

Recommended reading

If possible, before you leave home go to your local bookshop and purchase a selection of the following books:

Dictionaries and language books:
A small pocket English–Japanese/Japanese–English dictionary is best. Be sure to pick one with the Japanese portions written in the Roman alphabet (which the Japanese call Romaji), not Kanji (Chinese-style) ideograms. A table that translates Japanese Hirigana and Katakana alphabets into their Romaji phonetic equivalents is helpful if you want to try deciphering Japanese words on signs or brochures.

A phrasebook is only useful if you really intend to study the language. You can ask questions with a phrasebook, but will you understand the answers? I've included some phrases in the back of this book, and most dictionaries have a phrase section. There are plenty of phrasebooks for sale in Japan if you should feel yourself desperately in need of one.

The best books for English-speakers to gain insight into subtleties of the Japanese language and culture are a series of slim volumes called *Nihongo Notes* by Osamu Mizutani and Nobuko Mizutani, published by The Japan Times Ltd., and widely available in Japan. These books (*Speaking and Living in Japan, Expressing Oneself in Japanese, Understanding Communication in Japanese*, etc.) are compiled from a daily column in *The Japan Times*, an excellent English-language newspaper found in most Japanese cities.

Guidebooks:
Purchase a comprehensive guidebook as a companion to this one. Of the many on the market, Fodor's and Baedecker's remain, in my opinion, the best. *Japan in Your Pocket* provides an itinerary for a true insider's look at Japan. It's the skeleton on which you hang the muscle and add the character. I won't tell you why the Daibutsu, the great Buddha, holds his fingers like that. Fodor's will.

Each guidebook has its own distinctive format and style. Browse through them at the bookshop and find one that you'd like to live with for a month. If you leave home without a guidebook, you'll find a good selection in Maruzen and Kinokuniya bookstores in major Japanese cities.

Some of the best places we'll visit on this itinerary are only mentioned briefly (or not at all) in most "comprehensive" guidebooks. Supplement your library with the English-language info readily available at Japan's Tourist Information Centres.

General background reading:
A painless way to learn about Japanese culture, customs and history is to spend spare moments both before and during your trip reading a novel set in Japan. A couple of suggestions . . .

Lafcadio Hearn wrote of turn-of-the-century Japan in a series of short story collections, novels and essays of which the most readily available is *Writings from Japan* (Penguin Books).

Works by two of Japan's greatest 20th century literary figures, Mishima Yukio (*The Sea of Fertility Tetralogy, The Sailor Who Fell from Grace with the Sea*) and Yasumari Kawabata (*Beauty and Sadness, The Master of Go*, and *Snow Country* which takes place in a traditional Japanese inn) are available in inexpensive paperback English language translations.

The Japan National Tourist Organisation will send you lots of good literature free for the asking. Their address and telephone number are given at the back of the book.

Don't panic!
Watch your mental attitude: Before my first trip to Japan, as one of a group of 24 college students, our group leader made us read a short article on 'culture shock' — an emotional rejection of a culture based on subconscious fear (xenophobia) laced with homesickness.

After the first weeks of home life with Japanese families in the industrial environs of Osaka, all the members of our group found ourselves in a constant state of mental malaise. The reasons? Everything from curfew at our Japanese homes, to just too much Japanese food. Our leader called a group meeting one afternoon after school and told us point-blank that we were all suffering from 'culture shock'. Ah, Baloney!, we cried as one, but then, words faintly remembered from the article he'd made us read came drifting back, and I thought, 'I'm acting like the ignorant specimen I vowed never to be'. Recognising the problem was all it took to get every one of us back on track. Soon we were enjoying Japan and the families we were staying with like never before.

If you wake up one morning seething mad because you've been served sea slug for breakfast once too often, remember: your hosts think you like sea slug! You have only to explain that you would really rather have a fried egg and toast, and you'll get it.

In this three-week trip, you'll see more of Japan than the average so called Japanologist does in his one or two year stay. To absorb and fully enjoy it requires a willingness to see, feel and experience without comparing it to "back home". (There will be plenty of time later to compare aspects of your everyday life to what you discovered in Japan.) The Japanese *are* different, as we are to them — sometimes maddeningly so. Relax. Somehow they've managed just fine for thousands of years, and rest assured they'll keep right on doing so after you've gone. The more you can let go and get into the culture, the more you'll get out of the experience. If you read up beforehand, you'll waste less energy being astounded by new behaviour and you'll be better able to experience and appreciate it.

Learn a few words of Japanese. Yes, of course it's a fairly difficult language, but so what? Don't worry about your accent — just say it. People from Tokyo poke fun at the merchants' accent from Osaka, too; the typical Osaka greeting, "Mo karemaka?" ("Making any money?") is good for a laugh most places outside of Osaka.

A simple greeting in Japanese will loosen up everyone in the little bar or teashop you happen to drop into. Remember that many Japanese, particularly in the countryside, *have never seen a foreigner*! Don't be excessively noisy, but don't be shy either.

If you catch the fellow at the end of the bar staring at you, don't get upset — talk to him. He's curious, not rude. He knows about Gaijin (foreigners) mainly from TV and print media — usually as beautiful models enjoying the good life and selling something. Now, into his local coffee shop steps the real thing. Wouldn't you be curious? Dare to communicate with him!

BASIC TRAVEL HINTS

Packing

What to take is the eternal question for travellers. If you could travel in the 'old style' it would be no problem. You would have several steamer trunks full of all that life might require and armies of helpful bearers to lug it all around for you. No such luck in modern Japan, though. All the money in the world won't get you a porter on a crowded morning in Ueno Station. Japan is a very egalitarian sort of place when it comes to luggage — every man for himself (women, too).

You'll often see Japanese people, masters at the art of packing light, who set out on long journeys with a bare minimum of belongings. Personally, I prefer the luxury of a few changes of clothing. A fine balance is called for: enough stuff to wear and be comfortable without creating an un-luggable burden.

I strongly recommend convertible luggage that can be carried as a back pack or as a suitcase. The shoulder straps and hip harness typically zip inside when you want to carry the bag by its handle. It's much easier to carry forty pounds on your back than in your hand, yet when checking into a nice hotel or ryokan, you can zip up the straps, leave the vagabond look out on the sidewalk, and check in with dignity. Look for sturdy construction, a main compartment that opens wide so you don't have to 'stuff' your clothes, and a good backpack suspension system. How many external pockets you want is up to you. I carry a bag on which the large outside pocket zips off and becomes a day pack.

When packing, consider the time of year you'll be going. The only thing you'll use a heavy sweater for in the summer is a pillow.

My Dad's favourite saying was, 'Travel light and carry enough money to buy what you need when you get there'. This philosophy has its drawbacks, though. While you can get just about anything you need in Japan, men especially will have a hard time finding large sizes in clothing and shoes. A Japanese size 'LL' (extra large) is a UK 'Medium'. Size 10 shoes are virtually non-existent.

Obviously you'll find items like toothpaste, shampoo and soap everywhere. Try new brands. The Japanese have some of the best cosmetics in the world.

Carry any prescription medicines you may need in sufficient quantity for the trip and a bit extra. If you wear contact lenses, carry spares (although I understand Japan is the place to buy good lenses). Any personal hygiene items you are particularly fond of should be carried along, although you will be able to find substitutes if necessary.

Take a couple of small plastic bottles, available at camping stores, to keep soap and detergent in. You will be doing your own laundry often as not. In the cities it is easy enough to find laundries, but out in the country, you'll be using the facilities offered by the inns where you're staying.

Carry more socks than you think you'll ever need.

Carry fewer 'dress-up' clothes than you think you need. Carry some nice evening clothes, but be casual. Your hosts won't expect you to have a suit or evening gown.

Carry one or at most two pairs of shoes. Try and find an attractive walking shoe you could bear to go out at night in, too.

Carry a good *light* raincoat, a coated nylon raincoat. Rain in Japan differs from ours. It's soft and warm except in winter, requiring minimal protection. Everyone uses umbrellas, cheap and readily available at umbrella racks everywhere.

Use layers of clothing for cold weather versatility. Unless you plan to go to Hokkaido in winter, leave out the parka. On the other hand, a down vest packs small and is ideal in an emergency cold spell.

Take along a small cheap compass to help you follow maps and directions in this book. A small Swiss Army knife with a can opener, tweezers and tooth pick is invaluable.

Pack early — days early. Think about distributing your load so that it will carry nicely and you can find things without groping through your laundry all the time. Pick up your kit and walk a half mile with it. Can you do it? If not, lighten the load. You will get in better shape during the trip, and what seemed heavy at the beginning will seem light at the end; but start light so you can add goodies en-route, avoiding the effort and expense of sending purchases home from overseas.

Getting there
Check with your travel agent for the best flight deal to Japan. Prices can range from £650 for the return ticket at the lower end of the scale, to over £1,200. First class would of course be extra, and you should book well in advance. Departures for Japan are generally in the afternoon.

Accommodation
Unless you want to risk travelling unreserved (it can be done, but not always easily), make reservations in advance through the **Tokyo Minshuku Centre,** the only organisation that will reserve you rooms across the country in the small family-run minshuku and pensions I recommend in this book. Asano-san, the director of the Centre, speaks English quite well. He can help you select

good alternatives if any of the inns I recommend are booked up. Send him a clearly written itinerary at least a month in advance of your arrival, and you will have all your reservations in hand by the second day of your trip, if not before you even leave home. The address is: Tokyo Minshuku Centre, Kotsu Kaikan Bldg. 2-10-1 Yurakucho, Chiyoda-ku, Tokyo. Tel: (03) 216-6556.

Most of my recommendations for accommodation fall into two categories, both of which will also provide your morning and evening meals:

Ryokan: Traditional Japanese inns which observe and respect the virtues and beauties of old Japan. The building may not be much to look at from outside, the lobby may be somewhat modern in style, but the spirit will always be traditional. You will often be greeted by a wetted entryway to show welcome. Your room will have tatami mats on the floor, a tokonoma (alcove) for flowers, and austere decoration in the traditional manner. The futons (beds), stored in a cupboard, will be made for you in the evening, usually while you are in the o-furo (bath) or taking a stroll after dinner. Bathrooms may be in the room but more often, in reasonably priced ryokan, they will be down the hall. There is usually a separate area for brushing teeth and face washing. You will often have a lady in waiting, dressed in kimono, to serve you. Typical ryokan food is kaiseki ryori (see the section on Food), served in your room or in a dining room downstairs.

Minshuku: Minshuku ordinarily cost less than ryokan (though the rates for both vary widely in different areas of the country), and have less personalised service. There's little difference between an *exceptionally good* minshuku and an *average* ryokan. Sometimes the minshuku will be the nicer place; the ones on the Izu Peninsula for example, are very fine and offer a degree of comfort and service unmatched by many ryokan that cost much more. In minshuku you eat in a common dining room instead of the privacy of your own room, and you make up your own bed in the evening. Be polite and pick up your futon in the morning. If you have trouble making the bed or just don't know how, say 'Futon o oshienasai' (literally, "Show me the futon" — not great Japanese, but it will get the idea across).

Note: All prices are quoted per person, with two meals, except at the New Otani Hotel. You may find that you don't like Japanese breakfasts. If so, you can save from 500 to 1,000 yen (£2.25 to £4.50) daily by telling the innkeeper, 'Asa gohan wa irimasen,' I won't be having breakfast. Generally it is easier just to request toast and coffee. It will be cheaper than eating breakfast out.

When staying in either minshuku or ryokan, please observe the rules of etiquette fundamental in Japan. Proving that you're not a barbarian will ensure warm welcomes not only for you but also for other travellers who follow in your footsteps. For instance:

Baths (o-furo): *Wash off first, then get in.* They are usually very hot. Do not reduce the temperature in a bath unless you are the last one in. If you can't bear it, tell the host 'O-furo wa chotto atsu sugimasu' ('This tub is a little too hot') and perhaps they will tone it down for you. Reheat the water before you leave the room.

In places with a hot spring-fed tub (known as 'onzen') you may not be able to get in unless your temperature tolerance level far exceeds that of a lobster. If it's a large bath, you may not do anything about it at all if someone is already in it. In small, spring fed tubs the temperature will recoup automatically, so it may be okay to cool it down a little at first. Make it bearable, but not so comfortable that you could stay in for a long time. If someone else comes along, they'll want it really hot.

Slippers: Wearing slippers indoors keeps the tatami mats on the floor clean. Shoes that have been worn outside *must not* be worn past the entranceway. The same applies to the wooden slippers provided for you to wear outside. There are separate slippers for the bathroom, too. In some nice clean places these are more a formality than a necessity, but in others the reason for them will quickly become apparent. Don't wear them out of the bathroom. Don't enter any room with tatami mats on the floor wearing any shoes or slippers unless they're provided at the doorway. The foremost concern of many ryokan and minshuku managers is whether foreign guests can be relied upon to observe their civilised customs, particularly those regarding footwear. (Speaking of feet, never clip toenails or fingernails in public; if you do so in private carefully dispose of the clippings, which the Japanese find unutterably disgusting.)

Tipping: In ryokan a small gratuity to the maid is customary. Don't hand over cash, though; this is considered very rude. Wrap your gift in paper, even facial tissue if nothing better is at hand. Tipping is not necessary in minshuku. If someone is particularly nice to you, buy them a box of candy at a store to show your appreciation, and have it wrapped.

Breakfast: By asking ahead of time you can nearly always get toast and coffee for breakfast if you'd prefer not to start the day with cold salted fish and rice with a seaweed relish. You may learn to love the Japanese breakfast — at least parts of it such as the rice or miso shiro soup — but few foreigners are wild about raw egg for breakfast.

No smoking areas: The Shinkansen have them, as do larger ferry boats (ask for a 'kinnen-sha' when you get your tickets). Elsewhere... bring your respirator. Though attitudes are changing and some Japanese people are cutting down or at least switching to milder brands, overwhelming numbers of the Japanese are still very much committed to their tobacco habits. Many jokingly refer to smoking as their hobby!

Japan rail pass

You'll need one of these. Public transport is the only sensible way to go in Japan. Driving, with some few exceptions, is too difficult and expensive.

A rail pass will save you a lot of money and time at ticket windows. There are two classes besides child fares. Second class are fine seats, but they can be a bit cramped for large Gaijin frames. If you can manage the extra cost I recommend first class. The seats are much more comfortable, your fellow passengers are much more reserved and their children are quieter. You'll arrive at your destination ready to do something other than search for peace and quiet.

A 21-day second-class pass is 55,000 yen (£250); the first-class pass is 78,000 yen (£355). The passes are good on Bullet Trains, expresses and ferry boats as well as buses and other transport run by Japan Railways (JR).

You must buy an exchange order for your Japan Rail Pass before you leave home. Your travel agent should be able to arrange one for you. If not, contact the Japan Travel Bureau or the Japan National Tourist Organisation (phone numbers are given at the back of the book). Passes are also available from Compass, 46 Albemarle Street, London W1X 4EP (Tel: 01-408 4141).

Activating your rail pass: After clearing customs upon your arrival at Narita Airport, take your rail pass exchange order to the JTB office at the airport and receive the actual pass. A taxi to the centre of town would cost around 12,000 yen (£55). If you intend to stay longer than three weeks in Japan, you're better off taking a regular bus into town and waiting to activate your pass until you're really ready to hit the old Tokkaido Road (Japanese for "dusty trail") out of Tokyo on Tour 4. You can activate it then at the JTB travel agency by the main doors adjacent to the ticket office at Tokyo Station; allow an extra half hour.

Subways

In Tokyo, the subway is the way to get around. Avoid the early morning and late afternoon rushes — mid-day is frantic enough. If you must see how tightly packed humans can get, go down to Ueno Station at 7:30 am.

Getting around central Tokyo is easy enough, as most station signs are written in English as well as Japanese. Buying the correct ticket is the first challenge. One way to get the right ticket is to go to the Fare Adjustment window (midori-no madoguchi), say the name of your destination and hand over what you're sure must be enough money (maybe 300 yen (£1.35); remember, these people are totally honest). Another, perhaps easier, way is to buy the cheapest ticket, then go to the Fare Adjustment window when you reach your destination and pay the balance due. Try asking passers-by how much to wherever you're going; you may get lucky and find an English speaker.

The next challenge is to get on the right train, and then get off at the right station. The following method works beautifully: simply smile and walk up to a likely-looking native holding your ticket and body in a questioning attitude. Say the name of your destination slowly and carefully. If they answer in Japanese and you can't understand, shrug and say 'Gaijin-des' (pron: guy-jean-des: 'I'm a foreigner'). The least you'll get is pointed in the right direction, and often you'll be led by the hand to the right track. The most likely people to ask for directions are 13- to 18-year-old schoolgirls. You may only get giggles, but there's a good chance you'll have a 'would like to practise English' guide on your hands.

By the time you've used the Tokyo subways a bit, the rest of this trip will seem easy. Acting friendly and lost will get you an amazing amount of help. Often, particularly in rural areas, just the lost questioning posture will prompt some citizen to try and help you out.

Taxis

Taxis are temptingly easy to use. Once in a while, they're great; using them all the time will eat a huge hole in your budget. Take a taxi if you need to get somewhere in a hurry, if you're too tired to deal with the subway, or if you're desperate for an air-conditioned ride around town. Also it's quite possible you'll be out late one night after the other public transport systems have shut down (11 pm or midnight in most cities).

A red light in the window indicates that the taxi is free (green light means it's occupied or reserved). Some places, such as train stations, have taxi stands — you must get in line and wait your turn. Elsewhere, just wave one down on the street. Hold your hand up with your palm flat. If you hold up one finger, it means you're willing to pay the flat rate. Two fingers out means you'll pay double. In extreme emergencies hold out three fingers — but at this rate, believe me it's *much* cheaper to wait a while longer.

The more polite, clean and respectable you look, the easier it will be to get a taxi.

Taxi rates go up 20% after 11 pm, and there is a time charge in slow traffic.

When boarding a taxi, never try to open your own door. The left rear door is opened and closed mechanically by the driver. Don't do it yourself or you'll mess up all the little levers and doodahs the driver uses. Don't worry, he'll let you out when it's safe to do so. Exit only on the left side. Tipping is not necessary, and I don't unless a driver has been especially helpful or waited around a lot at no charge.

Buses

Travelling by bus is less fun than other transport modes, but it's sometimes the only way to get to the more secluded areas (hitchhiking excluded). Luggage is difficult to handle on buses, so try and get on board early and stow your stuff in the back of the bus.

The fares are usually posted on a revolving schedule at the front of the bus. Often, if you get on at the train station that will be square one on the fare system and you'll pay the highest fare on the list. Be sure to have correct change at hand when you get off so that you don't keep everyone waiting. On most buses you drop your coins onto a little conveyor belt arrangement as you get off; there may be a note-changer next to the belt, but there usually isn't.

Boats and ferries

Ferry and boat terminals are set up similarly to all other public transport in the country. You will normally have no trouble figuring out how to get where you're going. Many boat lines are privately run and your JR pass won't work. Don't worry — most are quite reasonably priced.

Car hire

You will only hire cars twice on this suggested itinerary (Karatsu and Sado), and if you prefer not to drive you can get by with buses instead.

Hiring a car is easy. You must have an International Drivers Licence (get one from an AA office) and a major credit card. Cars can be hired with cash only, but the rent-a-car man will feel better if you show him a credit card. Cars can be rented on an hourly basis, so if you should decide at any point that you need a car for a morning, go ahead and get one. The most easy-to-find agency is Eki Rent-A-Car, with offices in front of most major and many minor train stations.

Driving: If you're slow and careful, you will have no trouble driving in the places I have suggested you hire a car — country and small town areas where the traffic is usually light. My advice is, don't hire in the larger cities. To a Gaijin it looks like sheer vehicular mayhem out on the streets of Tokyo. (In actuality, the Japanese drive far more skilfully than we do because the traffic moves faster on unbelievably narrow lanes that don't even have shoulders.)

The Japanese drive on the left, as in the UK. Take it slow and think where you're going to turn and which lane to turn into. Be particularly careful when you enter a traffic-free street.

The other main difficulty is navigating when you can't read the street signs. Again, this is not too bad in the country but very scary in big cities. Try to commit a roadmap to memory, and if possible have a passenger navigate for you.

Do not drink and drive in Japan. They are as serious as a heart attack about that offence! Keep your speed down, drive carefully, use common sense and you should have no problems.

Money

The unit of currency in Japan is the yen. Prices given in this book are in yen with the approximate sterling equivalent in brackets, based on about 220 yen to the pound.

Many places don't accept credit cards. Small restaurants and inns in the country seldom accept them. Still, a credit card will sometimes smooth your way. The American Express Card lets you get cash advances at their service banks in major Japanese cities. Visa and Mastercard (Access) are more widely accepted in Japan, and you can often get cash advances on these too. A credit card will also make car hire easier.

Travellers cheques are widely accepted in Japan. Use them as a safe vehicle for your money (about the only thieves in Japan I'm ashamed to say, are foreigners), but not for purchases. Exchange them for yen at a bank and pay cash whenever possible to minimise service charges.

Change money at banks — their exchange rate will usually be slightly better than at hotels. Most banks in cities and larger towns have a foreign exchange window or desk; transactions are handled efficiently and quickly.

Vouchers and meal tickets are quite common. For example, when you make reservations at the Minshuku Centre, you will receive vouchers for ryokan, minshuku and hire car. You'll exchange them instead of paying cash, and nothing else is needed.

Similarly, in many restaurants — notably soba ya or noodle shops — you pay for your meal first and receive a ticket. Recognise these by noticing if the cashier has a large box of plastic or wooden tokens that he or she is giving out, or if people are buying tickets at a machine before approaching the counter.

ITINERARY

TOUR 1 After a long flight you'll arrive in Tokyo at almost the same time of day as you left home.

TOUR 2 Confirm your travel arrangements for the trip, then see some of Tokyo's sights. Stop for lunch at a wonderful little noodle shop, and explore your new country.

TOUR 3 This is a day to rest, recoup travel-worn resources and see more of Tokyo. Save some energy for the Kabuki-za theatre and the glittering Ginza this evening.

TOUR 4 Leaving Tokyo, travel by Bullet Train to the Izu Peninsula, then by train and bus through beautiful coastal scenery on the way to historic Shimoda. Spend your first night in a traditional Japanese minshuku in Toi.

TOUR 5 Near your accommodation, view the coastal sights including Mt Fuji, the seascapes of Matsuzaki and the gorgeous orchids at Dogashima as well as the troublesome monkeys at Hagachi. Rest and really get over the jet-lag. Do only as you please. Maybe the beach is where you belong today.

TOUR 6 Today you'll see how well Japan's travel network really works — ten boat, taxi, train and bus rides in six hours. Long but fun, with enthralling views. The views of the Izu Peninsula coastline, the Atsumi Peninsula and the Mikawa bay are breathtakingly scenic. Meet some country folks who don't see Gaijin every day. Practise your phrasebook Japanese.

TOUR 7 Visit Japan's greatest national shrines. The Geku and the Naiku at Ise are the seat of Shintoism, Japan's own religion. Their grand, pure Japanese architecture will give you a real feeling for the ancient culture of Japan. Evening will find you in everyone's favourite Japanese city, Kyoto.

TOUR 8 Explore the temples, shrines, labyrinthine alleys and shops on the eastern hillsides of Kyoto. Your feet will be all the transport you'll need this morning. See the imposing Nijo Castle in the afternoon and visit the very Japanese Gion district for evening enjoyment.

TOUR 9 Take a side trip to Nara today to round out your

education in classical Japanese architecture and history. Nara's temples are among the finest in the country and rank with the shrines at Ise in cultural importance. So much to see and do that the day will be gone before you know it.

TOUR 10 Today you're off to Shikoku, smallest of the main islands, and perhaps the least known to foreigners. Stop along the way at Himeji city to see the Shirasagi-jo castle, a feudal masterpiece. Continue across the Inland Sea to Shikoku and the small town of Kotohira. Climb the longest staircase you've ever seen (you'll love it) and see the Kompira Shrine, sacred to Japanese mariners.

TOUR 11 Travel the length of Shikoku on a comfortable train and cruise through the finest neck of the Inland Sea on an even nicer boat to the gorgeous island of Miyajima. The evening will be free to stroll around one of the three most beautiful islands in Japan.

TOUR 12 Feel free to relax and enjoy this splendid little island any way you please. Early morning might find you nearly alone watching the sun paint the famous red Torii in front of your ryokan. Walk all or part of the island's circumference. Have a tea lunch in Momijidani, the maple valley.

TOUR 13 After a morning at the sombre and sobering Peace Park in Hiroshima, buy a lunch in a small bakery to eat while the Bullet Train whisks you south to the island of Kyushu. Arriving at Karatsu, hire a car for a drive out of the peninsula to Hatomisaki and Yobuko town.

TOUR 14 Drive around the peninsula and explore tiny narrow bays and inlets, with jewel-like villages nestled down in narrow canyon bottoms. Today is casual. Visit the rural morning market in Yobuko. If you want to sleep late, go ahead and sleep. The day is yours.

TOUR 15 Back to the big city of Kyoto. By now you'll probably feel at home in your accommodation here, so you'll have no trouble entertaining yourself. There's a lot of Kyoto you haven't even been near yet, so wander around unfettered and discover your own favourite corner of this captivating city.

TOUR 16 Travel by train to the western coast, a region of intriguingly different scenery and friendly people. Enjoy a low-key, high-class corner of the land. The Gardens at Kanazawa are among the finest anywhere.

TOUR 17 Today is a long travel day. Again, the sights en route more than make up for your pains. You will see the west coast of Japan through the window of an excellent train while enjoying regional specialities packed in keepable containers for lunch. From Niigata to the island of Sado you'll be lulled by the sound of the Sea of Japan.

TOUR 18 Explore Sado as you drive yourself around an island so exotic-looking you'll think you've been transported into an ancient oriental landscape painting. Pass one breathtaking view and charming coastal town after the other on your way to friendly little Negai.

TOUR 19 Return by Boeing Jet-Foil to Niigata, then climb into the breathtaking mountains of central Honshu aboard an old (but comfortable) diesel train. You'll pass village after village to which you'd love to return.

TOUR 20 Nearing the end of the trip, you'll see one of the most colourful shrines in all Japan. Admire the shrines of Nikko and the natural beauty of the lake and mountains around nearby Chuzenji. Wind up your day with a quiet evening 'at home' in your ryokan, minshuku or pension, or a stroll around the romantic waters of the clear cold lake.

TOUR 21 Today brings a bumper crop of sights. Take the bus back down the hill to Nikko's Toshogu Shrine. A riot of colour and intricate architecture awaits you here along with the original 'Hear No Evil, See No Evil, Speak No Evil' monkeys. Nikko will make you feel like you're getting back on the beaten path, but you'll be a changed person — a traveller of Japan.

TOUR 22 Time to complete the loop. A two-hour ride will return you to the starting point of your holiday. Revisit old haunts or explore a part of the city you missed the first time through. Rest up for tomorrow's flight back home. You won't forget this trip. I promise!

TOUR 1

HELPFUL HINTS

Depending on your starting point, this could be a very long day. Be sensible and the trip won't take all the wind out of your sails.
- Rest well the night before your departure.
- Carry a toothbrush and a fresh shirt or blouse to avoid that crumpled feeling on arrival.
- Wear loose, comfortable clothing and shoes on the flight. Carry a light, warm sweater or jacket.
- Sleep as much as possible on the plane. If you see an empty row in the middle of the plane, occupy it immediately. Four seats to sleep on beat first class for comfort.
- Take a Walkman with language tapes, music or a book on tape. Several hours on a commercial jetliner can seem like weeks.

ARRIVE IN TOKYO

Suggested schedule
Arrive at Narita Airport.
Two hour bus ride to the centre of town.
Check into your hotel.
Gather your strength and get out on the town for a while.

Customs will seldom open your bags and you'll soon be out on the street. Trade your pounds for yen at one of the several bank-operated currency exchanges in the airport lobby. The Tourist Information Centre (TIC), also in the lobby, can provide you with free maps, transport schedules and hotel information. Be sure to get a map of Tokyo, Tokyo Walking Tour brochures and any other literature that looks useful.

Although you're probably tired after the long daylight flight, you still have a two-hour bus ride ahead. Airport limousine buses will leave you at the Tokyo City Air Terminal in the centre of town, with easy access to the subway system. Airport express buses will take you to major hotels in the central area, including the New Otani. Both limousine and express buses leave frequently from in front of the arrival lounge.

The cheapest way to get to the centre is the Keisei Skyliner Train, leaving from Keisei Airport Station.

If you want to activate your JR rail pass now, you can also take a JR train into town. Take the shuttle bus to nearby Narita Station where the train will take you to Tokyo Station. If you intend to stay in Japan more than three weeks, then you should pay for the ride into town and save your pass for real travelling.

When you arrive in town, take the subway or a taxi to your lodgings. If it's anywhere near rush hour, avoid taking the subway with luggage.

Orientation

Tokyo is truly vast. The only quick way in and out of town is the Bullet Train, and even that takes time. Entire guidebooks are written about Tokyo alone.

Get out the map of Tokyo you picked up at the airport TIC and have a look at the general layout of the city. Tokyo is made up of wards and neighbourhoods; the Ginza, Asakusa, Ueno, Akasaka, Shinjuku and Akihabara are the most interesting to first-time visitors. Each has its own distinctive character. Kasumigaseki is the commercial district. Akihabara is where you'll find electronic products. The Ginza has expensive shopping and entertainment. Roppongi is where Gaijin and young Japanese go to cavort. Shinjuku offers brilliantly lit, commercial, fun and sometimes seedy nightlife. Tsukiji is for fish, food and cookware shopping. Akasaka's nightlife quarter, fun for all, defies categorisation. Ueno and Asakusa are loaded with shopping, museums, a zoo, temples and more.

Even more so than London or New York, Tokyo would take several lifetimes to really get to know — by the time you got to the end you'd find that the beginning needed sorting out again. It is hectic and crowded beyond belief; but it is also safe, fun, energetic in the extreme and constantly changing. Learn it a bit and you'll love it.

Accommodation

Tokyo has literally thousands of places to stay, ranging in price from cheap to absurd. Small interesting places are scarce and usually expensive. Ryokan, common elsewhere, are rare in the city. The rule is large western style hotels, of which there are many in all price ranges. The larger and more famous places such as the Okura, the New Otani and the Takanawa Prince are elegant to varying degrees and commensurately expensive.

The New Otani: Central location, vast facilities and a good members' discount. Ask your travel agent at home to inquire about a New Otani Club membership for you. It gives you a 10% cost break and entitles you to free breakfasts in a choice of

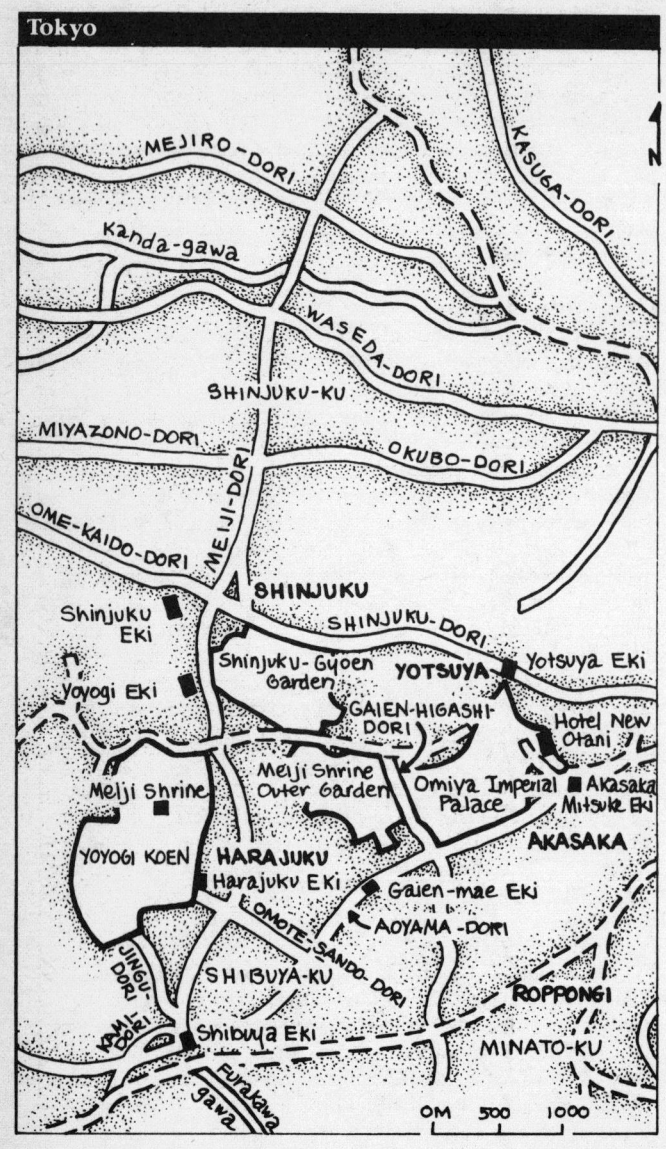

Tour 1

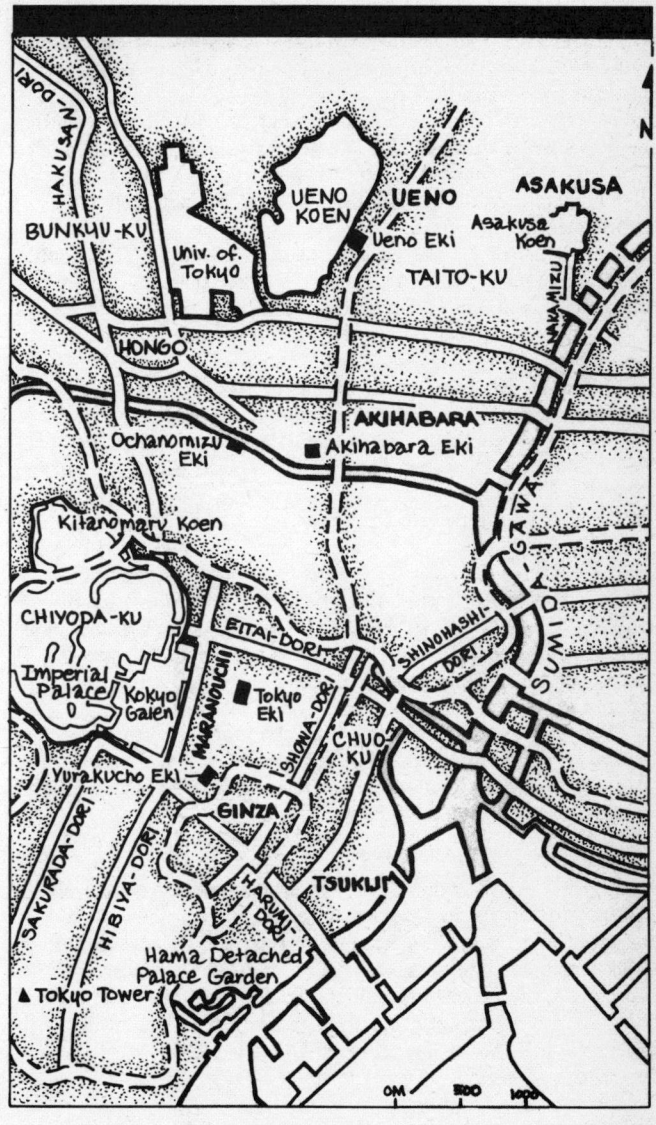

restaurants with great views of the city and the fabulous New Otani Gardens. The membership takes a couple of weeks to process, so apply well in advance. The New Otani has a good place to leave luggage if you decide to take a side trip, good subway coverage with both Yotsuya and Akasaka Mitsuke stations in easy walking distance, and the greatest health club in the world for guests' use. Avoid room service and laundry and you'll be able to sleep two for around 18,000 yen (£80) including complimentary breakfast.

Many small hotels are available in the 13,000 yen (£60) double occupancy range. Primarily for businessmen, they are usually not much to look at and lack character. One of the best is the **Hokke Club,** quietly located near Ueno's Zoo and Museums. Tel: 834-4131.

TaiEiKan Ryokan, in the Hongo area of Ueno near Tokyo University, is traditional Japanese style inside and out. The service is personable and the breakfast is raw. At 5,500 yen (£25) per person with breakfast the price is very reasonable for Tokyo. Tel: (03) 811-6226.

Boarding with a private family household near Tokyo is an inexpensive option if you have extra time. Asano-san and his helpers at the Minshuku Centre can arrange it for you. This is the best way to get 'inside' the Japanese culture, and is usually arranged for one week duration, but overnights are available too. The cost for one week with a family is around 25,000 yen (£115) for a couple — a very good deal. Only outgoing, seriously interested persons should apply.

These are a small sampling of the many places to stay in Tokyo. If you would rather be in a specific area such as Akasaka, ask TIC or a JTB travel agent, or have your agent at home help you with arrangements.

Food

Eating in Tokyo is simple; just follow your nose. As you walk the streets you will see hundreds of interesting little places. The variety would easily fill a tome twice this size. Be adventurous. Stick your nose into doors. Be ready for all kinds of responses from a glad welcome to a solid stony silence at the appearance of a bizarre apparition (you). Many places advertise their wares with plastic replica food in the window. Don't hesitate to drag the waiter or proprietor out into the street as you point at your selection.

Tokyo has so many places foreigners haven't found yet that with enough exploring you could write your own book.

Good Tokyo Restaurants, by Rick Kennedy, is a great guide to eating and drinking in this town. The book is widely available in Japan.

A famous and delicious place for tonkatsu or pork cutlet is **San Kin,** on the corner west of the Yotsuya station. Reasonable, very good and filling.

Want sushi? Wander around Roppongi and find your own little place. There are a couple of good ones down the hill behind the Almond Cafe at the Roppongi Kossuten.

For a good late night dinner or snack I love the **Inakaya** in Roppongi. It's a £20 a head kind of place, but always good fun. This country-style inn, very popular with the Gaijin in town, sets everything in front of you, cooked to order. Try the asparagus, the potatoes and whatever else looks good. A cedar box full of sake called masuzake is a good way to get your meal rolling. It's across from the defence agency (Bo-e-cho) northwest of the Almond on the south side of Gaien-Higashi Dori.

If Indian food sounds good to you, try the **Taj** in Akasaka. Take the subway (chikatetsu) to Akasaka-Mitsuke Station. Come out from underground, head southeast on the main road, Sotobori-dori, for a few hundred yards and you're there. It's across the street from the Akasaka Tokyu Hotel, in case you still haven't found it.

Go back behind the Taj to find the Akasaka night life zone. A place called the **Tiger Bar** is on the second street in to the west, to the south of the station. Their happy hour, from 4:30 to 6:30, can't be beaten for price or beer quality. Appetisers are pricey.

Nightlife

You name it, they've got it. How much do you want to spend? Got a couple thousand (pounds!) for the evening's diversion? Go down to the Ginza and have a ball. If you're a little poorer, don't worry. There are still a few thousand places you can go; you can't go wrong. Pick your area for the kind of fun you want. The really happening places change from week to week, but a few are landmarks:

In Roppongi, find the **Lexington Queen, Giza** or **Tsubaki Ball.** They are all in the same area to the east of the Almond and south. Down at the south end of the quarter behind the Porsche dealer is a trendy new spot called **Cleo's.** Other hot places in the Roppongi area are **Masquerade** and **Les Choux,** down the hill towards Meguro.

Many Akasaka night clubs keep going forever. The names and locations remain the same while their clientele, decor and entertainment evolve. I recently revisited an old haunt called **Byblos** up the street from the Tiger Bar. Interesting. Young. . .

Have fun wandering the streets, talking to people both local and foreign, and just letting go. You can't get hurt in this town — except from alcohol poisoning or an extreme case of 'you've got to be kidding' when the bill comes. Seriously: Tokyo nightlife runs on affluent businessmen's expense accounts. A whisky can cost from £4 to £30 (880-6,600 yen) depending on the neighbourhood.

Have fun!

Helpful hints

Always plan to be doing something other than moving around during the morning and evening rush hours. Large subway stations such as Ueno and Tokyo turn into madhouses at those times.

Keep a map handy of whatever area you're in.

The TIC (Tourist Information Centre) can give you helpful information, maps and a wonderful service called Japan Travel Phone (call the operator and say "Collect call TIC") — English-speaking consultants for any problem or circumstance that might befall you in the city or out in the sticks. Teletourist, a taped 24 hour information service, is (03)-503-2911. Tokyo's main TIC office is at Kotani Bldg., 1-6-6 Yurakucho, Chiyodaku, tel: (03)-502-1461.

TOUR 2

EXPLORE TOKYO

Your only 'must-do' today is to confirm your travel arrangements. The rest of the day is free to see some of the sights at your leisure, visit a wonderful little noodle shop and explore a bit of Tokyo. Don't worry that you aren't seeing all the sights Tokyo has to offer. You'll get your fill of shrines and temples later on.

Suggested schedule	
	Early morning stroll around the neighbourhood.
8:00	Breakfast in your hotel.
9:30	Visit Minshuku Centre to pick up your reservations and coupons.
11:00	A stroll around Tenno Heka, the Imperial Palace, or the Bridgestone Museum.
13:00	Lunch at Yabu Soba.
14:00	Visit Akihabara.
16:00	Meiji Park for a restful stroll through 'real' Japan. Possibly walk through Harajuku on your way out of the park. If necessary, return to travel agency.
Evening	Early dinner and bed.

Getting to the Minshuku Centre

Take the subways to the Yurakucho Station. Immediately east of the station, in the basement of the Kotsu Kaikan Bldg., you will find the **Tokyo Minshuku Centre**, where you can make your lodging reservations for the trip (or pick them up if you wrote ahead).

Sightseeing highlights

● ● ● **Meiji Shrine/Park:** Built after the Emperor Meiji's death to honour the man who opened Japan to the world, this park is a haven of tranquillity — beautiful Shinto architecture and a peaceful environment in which to enjoy it. The large torii (gates) and the Iris Garden are particularly noteworthy. Try to be at the Kiyomasa Ido spring around closing time to sip crystal-pure water in a quiet, woody glade.

● **The Imperial Palace:** The Emperor's residence is not a major tourist experience. I'm sure that within are beautiful gardens, etc., but much like Buckingham Palace or the Oval

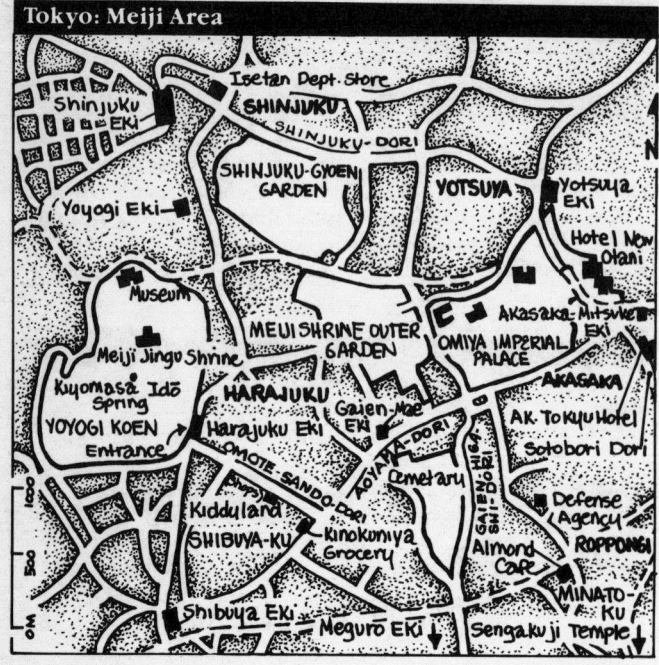

Office not just anyone gets to see them. Enjoy the grounds as much as you can and appreciate the stonework around the perimeter. You are in the centre of Tokyo here.

- **Transport Museum:** Next door to Yabu Soba, it is worth a visit on the way to Akihabara. A great collection of model trains, ships and planes and a glimpse of the building of modern Japan.
- **Akihabara:** Everything in the way of electronic wizardry Perhaps you need a 100-volt hair dryer that weighs only 4 oz, or a Walkman for the train. Yamagiwa, at the south end, has deals that a Gaijin should be happy with. The only places with better prices are in Shinjuku at Yodobashi Camera or Sakura Camera.
- **Harajuku:** Where the 'in' youth of Tokyo congregate, this neighbourhood is also popular with Gaijin. Stop at the Cafe de Rope for a coffee or beer. Next door up the street is Kiddyland, a five storey toy shop for kids of all ages.
- **Kinokuniya Grocers:** If you would like to take some western food such as ham, cheese or jam and cream along for a rolling picnic on the Shinkansen, this is the place to get it: a great international food store.

Transport

All of today's highlights are conveniently near subway stations, which in turn are found easily on the system map available at the TIC.

From the Minshuku Centre it is a five minute walk west to the Palace. From there, return to Yurakucho and take the Marunouchi Line to Ochanomizu. Stop for lunch at **Yabu Soba,** in a little walled enclosure behind the Kanda Post Office. If you say 'Yubin kyo ku wa doko deska' (Where is the Post Office?) someone will point you in the right direction.

After lunch, walk east and you can't miss Akihabara. The Transport Museum is on the way and on the map.

From Akihabara Eki, ride the JR line to Yoyogi, where you can walk or change for Meiji-jingu-mae. There you will find the Meiji Shrine.

To see Harajuku from the park, walk southeast a few hundred yards and you're there. The sights are all along Omote-sando dori; the grocery store is up at the top of the hill and a bit southwest on the main road.

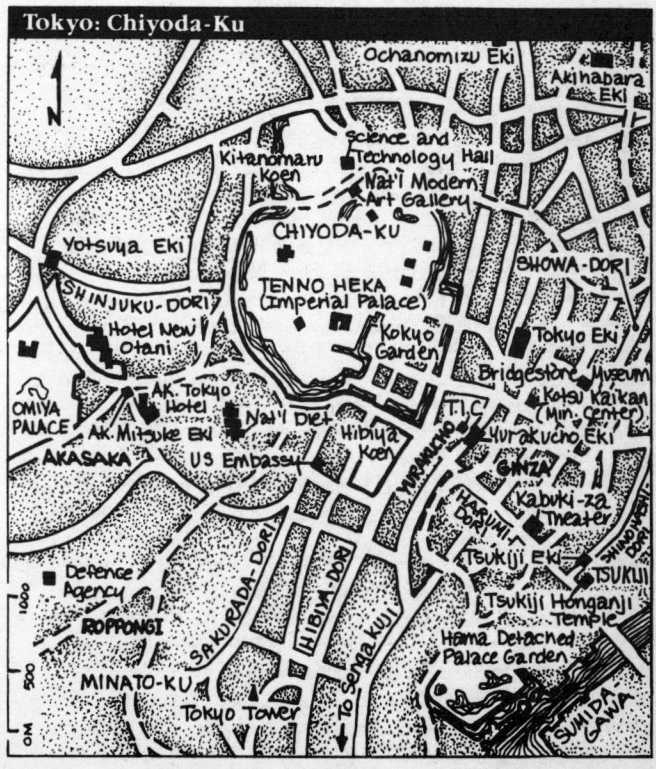

TOUR 3

MORE OF TOKYO

This is a day to rest, recoup faded bodily resources and see some more of Tokyo. You don't have to do everything on the suggested schedule. Go to the places that interest you or just go until you've had enough. Don't knock yourself out. Save some energy for the Kabuki-za theatre this evening.

Suggested Schedule

6:30	Tsukiji Fish Market.
8:00	Breakfast in your hotel.
9:00	Tokyo Tower for a view of the city.
10:00	Sengakuji.
11.30	Tsukiji for lunch — shushi-sashimi or soba.
12:30	Ginza for windowshopping.
13:30	Bridgestone Museum.
Afternoon	Ueno Park or Asakusa Shrine.
Evening	Kabuki Theatre and an evening out and about.

Sightseeing highlights

● ● ● **Tsukiji:** If you're an early riser, go down to Tsukiji Fish Market at first light (or before) to see more fish than one can even imagine in the ocean — a daily haul to feed one of the world's largest population centres. Almost all of Tokyo's fish comes from this neighbourhood. The action starts before daylight and is worth getting up early for. Join the fishmongers for an excellent and reasonably priced lunch (their dinner) in the neighbourhood. Don't worry; it's immaculate and doesn't even smell of fish. You'll find the market just to the south of Tsukiji stop on the Hibiya Line, in southeastern Tokyo.

● **Tokyo Tower:** If it's a clear day the Tower (a half-size replica of the Eiffel Tower) is worth a couple of hundred yen for the great panorama of the city it affords. Take your map up and familiarise yourself with the lay of the land. On a clear day you can see Mt Fuji.

● ● **Sengakuji:** The Temple of the 47 Ronin, the 47 masterless samurai. Revered as examples of true loyalty, these men gave their lives for their master who was wrongly sentenced to commit seppuku (ritual suicide, vulgarly called "harakiri"). It's a beautiful little temple, shrouded in mystery and reverential silence. A copy of the story in English is available from the shops at the temple entrance. The book makes good reading on the train or in ryokan and minshuku late at night.

- **The Ginza:** Some of the world's most valuable real estate — and the prices in the shops reflect it. You don't need to purchase anything, just have a lot of fun looking. Great toy shops and depaato (department stores). Look out for the Kabuki-za Theatre, where you may return tonight for a show. Maybe purchase your tickets now.
- **Kabuki-za Theatre:** Ginza: This famous theatre offers the fun spectacle of Kabuki with a distinct advantage for foreign tourists: English translations are available for a small charge. Kabuki come in two varieties; jidaimono and sewamono. Jidaimono is historical drama with great heroics and sacrifice in the traditional Japanese manner. Sewamono is intimate drama about common folk. In both types the main theme is conflict between one's duty and what one would like to do. Full of wild cross-eyed, swivel-necked theatrics, samisen music and clacking hyoshigi sticks, it is a uniquely Japanese art form that one should not miss. Admission ranges in price from 1,500 to 10,000 yen (£7 to £45) and the English Earphone Guide costs an additional 600 yen (£2.75). Daily matinee and evening performances.
- **The Bridgestone Museum:** Surely one of the best little museums anywhere. Renoir, Cezanne, Matisse, Degas and Picasso, as well as great Japanese artists, all in a little place you can easily see in an hour. Open daily from 10:00 am, admission 800 yen (£3.50).
- **Ueno:** Contains a great zoo, with what must be the most famous pandas in the world, along with several museums and galleries. You could easily spend all day here. Be sure to visit the zoo — great aviaries. If museums appeal to you, you could spend another day in the Tokyo National Museum and the Tokyo Metropolitan Art Gallery.
- **Asakusa-Kannon Temple:** A reconstruction of the original destroyed in World War II. The Sensoji Temple was begun by three 7th century fishermen who brought up a small statue of the Goddess of Mercy in their nets. Nakamise Street, the approach to the shrine, is typical of temple entranceways throughout the country. Enjoy the shops for their tradition and folk art. They're there to tempt the Japanese pilgrim as well as the foreign tourist. You might want to buy a good luck charm to ward off colds during your trip, or perhaps prayer beads. An incense burner in front of the shrine spews smoke that will cure what ails you. In front of the temples you'll find a fountain of water with long-handled bamboo cups. Rinse your hands and your mouth (spit the water out) in ritual cleansing before entering the temple.
- **Tea Ceremony (Chano-yu):** The traditional tea ceremony is an essential accomplishment for polite young Japanese women and an incomparable cultural experience for foreign visitors.

Tokyo: Ueno

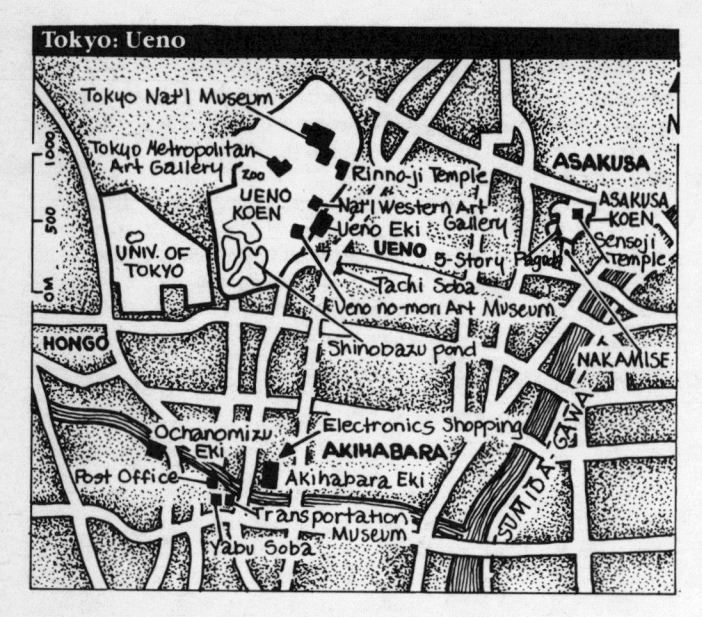

[Map showing Ueno area with landmarks: Tokyo Nat'l Museum, Tokyo Metropolitan Art Gallery, Zoo, Ueno Koen, Rinno-ji Temple, Nat'l Western Art Gallery, Ueno Eki, UENO, 5-Story Pagoda, Asakusa, Asakusa Koen, Sensoji Temple, Univ. of Tokyo, Tachi Soba, Ueno no-mori Art Museum, Hongo, Shinobazu pond, Nakamise, Ochanomizu Eki, Electronics Shopping, Akihabara, Post Office, Akihabara Eki, Transportation Museum, Yabu Soba, Sumida-gawa]

Several major Tokyo hotels, including the Imperial (504)-1111, the Okura (582-0111) and the New Otani (265-1111) feature afternoon demonstrations; reservations are required. Tea ceremony and flower arranging classes for foreign guests are held Thursdays and Fridays 11:00-15:00 at the Sakura-kai Tea Ceremony Centre (951-9403) in Shinjuku.

Food

Tsukiji, just a short hop from Sengakuji, has the best soba or sushi you've ever tasted. Try **Maruyo Soba,** a little stall just south on Shinohashi-Dori from Tsukiji-kossuten, the main crossing. Fantastic soba! Kakiyage-soba is noodles, broth and mixed veggies. Kakiyage-ten-soba is the same, with tempura shrimp thrown in. 'Shuniku Kudasai' gets you more watercress in your kakiyage. If you want added ingredients, just point. Cheap.

Or try **Takeno** restaurant. From the south corner of Tsukiji Honganji Temple turn left down Harumi-dori. Go down past the end of the temple. On the next block across the street you'll see several small alleys. Second from the southeast end is the one you want. Look for the phone number 541-8698 on the sign and you've got it. Great fish, cooked and raw, with or without rice, and excellent tempura.

In Ueno, you'll find a good stand-up noodle stall, **Tachi Soba,** under the train overpass to the right of Ueno station's north entrance. Very reasonable and the best broth anywhere.

Omote-sando: If you've got a craving for pizza made in Japan, go to the **Sabatini Pizzeria Romana.** Get off at the Gaienmae Eki stop of the Ginza Line and look for the big Suncrest building. In its basement is the pizzeria. Enjoy the food and the company — young Japanese, Italians and a scattering of Americans. 2,000 yen (£9) gets you dinner with room left over for an ice cream across the street at **Haagen-Dazs.**

Ikebukuro: For sake in a cosy-wild atmosphere, my newfound favourite is **Sasashu.** Difficult to find — detailed maps show me how to get there. Good luck. If you find it, you'll be glad you don't have to drive home.

TOUR 4

IZU PENINSULA – SHIMODA – TOI

Today you'll leave the modern madness of Tokyo on a journey around the Izu Peninsula, whose sheer-cliff seascapes, varied terrain and tumultuous history combine to create a beautiful first experience of rural Japan. Along the way, stop to visit a temple dedicated to the first US Ambassador's Japanese mistress, as well as an authentic Japanese country home. Tonight you'll stay in one of Japan's nicest minshuku.

Suggested schedule

8:21	Leave Tokyo Station (Eki) for Atami.
9:15	Change at Atami for Ito and continue south for Shimoda via Izu Kyuko Rensha and bus.
10:45	Arrive Shimoda.
11:30	Taxi from Shimoda Eki to Biragasu Mingekan.
2:00	Bus from Shimoda to Matsuzaki and change to bus to Toi.
3:30	Arrive in Toi, check into your minshuku.

The Izu Peninsula

Izu is the Japan you came to see: ragged rocky coasts, surging seas, winding ways and friendly locals. The Izu Peninsula is much loved by the Japanese for its natural majesty. Originally it was a place of exile for such notable Samurai as Minamoto Yoritomo and Sannetomo Minamoto. Their descendents are still here and their hokkori (pride) still abounds in the people of Izu today.

You are starting your journey in the same place that the original occidental (western) explorers did. Commodore Perry and the first US Ambassador to Japan, Townsend Harris, lived in Shimoda during the mid 1800s.

William Adams, a ship's pilot, lived here in the 1600s and built the first western style ship in Japan for the Tokugawa Shogun at the village of Ito. *Voila*, the plot of the book and TV movie *Shogun*!

While in Shimoda and Toi, notice the Tudor-like cross-hatched Namako-kabe architectural style, peculiar to this area.

Transport: Tokyo to Shimoda

Reread the section on basic travel methods over breakfast and try and be out early enough to miss the 7:30 am rush.

Tour 4

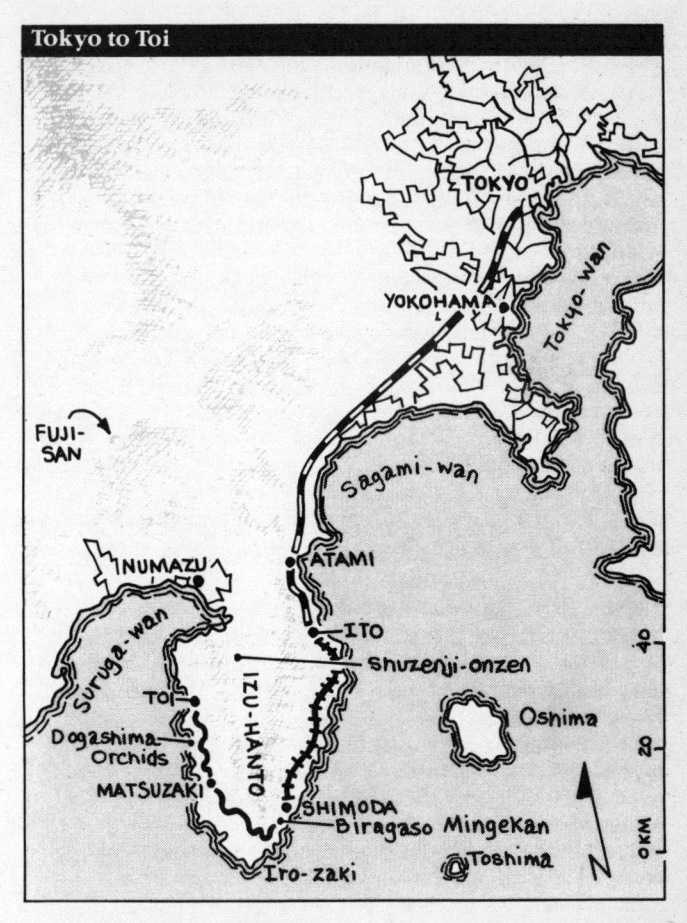

Tokyo to Toi

[Map showing the route from Tokyo to Toi, with labels: TOKYO, YOKOHAMA, Tokyo-wan, Fuji-san, Sagami-wan, NUMAZU, ATAMI, ITO, Shuzenji-onzen, Suruga-wan, TOI, IZU-HANTO, Dogashima Orchids, MATSUZAKI, Oshima, SHIMODA, Biragaso Mingekan, Toshima, Iro-zaki]

Take the subway to Tokyo Eki. You can activate your rail pass, if you haven't already done so, at the JTB office by the ticket office. The Bullet Train ticket window is in the middle of the station on the eastern side. It is a short ride to Atami; what you'll see out of the window is mostly urban sprawl.

At Atami, get to the ticket window again. Your rail pass will take you as far as Ito, where you must buy a ticket for the local, private train down the coast.

At Ito, change again for Shimoda. It's the same line and direction but a local (futsu rensha) train.

Sightseeing highlights — Shimoda

●● **Hofukuji Temple,** near the station, is worth a visit. It is dedicated to Okichi Tojin, the mistress of Townsend Harris. She was ordered by the Shogun to look after Harris. In the ensuing years, she and Harris became lovers. Like sailors since time immemorial, his tour of duty being up, he sailed back home to wife and family, leaving her with a broken heart and worse — much worse — the stigma of having been the first Japanese woman to fall for a Gaijin. Tainted and trapped by the conflict of cultures, she took the only possible recourse. She swam out to sea to drown.

● ● ● **Biragaso Mingekan:** An old-fashioned country home, a rarity in Japan, it is un-touristy and entirely authentic, with a thatched roof, tatami floors, indoor hearths and antique furnishings. It is the home of Dacky Murakami, alias Patito, a Renaissance man who speaks fluent Spanish, English, French and probably others. Ask him what 'ergonomy' is, and be sure and see his match-striker. For a small donation you're welcome to wander around to your heart's content. Don't get so wrapped up in his smoky little ante-room that you miss the other three floors of the house. A taxi driver will find the place easily for you and it is a cheap ride from the station.

Transport: Shimoda to Toi

After brief sightseeing and lunch, you'll find your bus from Shimoda to Matsuzaki at the train station. The buses can be crowded but the scenery along this route will more than reward you for your pains.

The town of Matsuzaki isn't much to look at, but its rugged sea-sculpted beaches certainly are. Have a look before you make the short bus ride up to Toi (pron: 'toy'). You may return here tomorrow.

At Matsuzaki, change buses to Toi. If you just say 'Toi, kudasai', in a curious questioning manner you will have no trouble getting on the right bus.

Arriving in Toi you're only a short walk away from your lodgings. From the bus station turn right up the hill across the bridge and turn right again. Down the hill is a park along the beach. Go south to the end of the park and you will come to a row of buildings. The Shio Kaze is the third building down. Next door is the Mihama.

Accommodation

Shio Kaze: Mrs Suzuki, who runs this minshuku, is like a mum if the house is not too crowded and you're a likeable sort. The excellent food and a room with a view of the waves lapping outside will leave no doubt that you're in the 'real' Japan. If you can reserve a corner room ('kado no heya'), do so. Tel:

05589-8-0740. Rooms cost from 4,000 to 7,000 yen (£18 to £32) with meals.

Mihama So: If you can't get a room at the Shio Kaze, get Mrs Suzuki to fix you up here, a five-second walk across the alley. The folks are very nice (the same family runs both places), the baths are large and the rooms clean. The ocean view is the same as at the Shio Kaze, and so are the prices.

Food and nightlife
John Lennon, the only bar in town, is next door to the Mobil Station and upstairs. Kanezashi Yoshio-san owns both the petrol station and the bar. Most evenings he can be found there amid the Beatle memorabilia. Though he speaks no English, he's a very friendly, helpful person. Show him your copy of *Japan in Your Pocket* please — he'll love it.

If you elect to eat out, there is a nice place up the main street about four doors from the petrol stand. The sushi is excellent and the kushikatsu (pork cutlet and egg with rice) is divine.

TOUR 5

TOI AND MATSUZAKI

View the sights, rest and really get over the jet-lag. Do only as you please. Maybe the beach is where you belong today. A short bus ride south will have you back in Matsuzaki, where you can walk and enjoy the extraordinary rock formations at your leisure. Further south by boat are the boisterous monkeys of Hagachi.

Suggested schedule

9:30	Walk along the beach for a while and see the town.
11:00	Take a bus (or walk) down the coast to see the Dogashima Orchid Centre and fantastic rock formations. Keep on the bus down the coast if you like.
13:00	From Matsuzaki, take a boat to Hagachi to see 'wild' monkeys romping on the cliffs.
Afternoon	Continue your tour of the peninsula or return for a swim in Toi.
Evening	Rest and recreate. Have a long bath in the lovely o-furo in your minshuku.

ALTERNATIVE: Visit Shuzenji-onzen for the day.

Sightseeing highlights

● ● ● **The scenery** of the coast. Matsuzaki, 2½ miles south of Toi, is well worth a visit, as are all the view points along the way. Bizarre rock formations. From many of these points you can see Mt Fuji as it is best seen: in the distance.

● **Dogashima Orchid Centre:** Great orchids, what can I say? On the way to Matsuzaki.

● **Hagachi-zaki:** Wild monkeys and more beautiful coastline. Watch your handbags, ladies — the monkeys are wild, all right. A 45-minute boat ride from Matsuzaki.

● ● **Shuzenji-onzen:** One of Japan's most famous hot-spring resorts — overbuilt, overpriced, but a fine resort. The Shuzenji Temple merits a visit. The tombs of Minamoto Yoritomo, founder of the Kamakura Shogunate, and his brother are here. The Shigetsuden Temple across the river from the tombs is a serene little gem. Buses run frequently all day from Toi.

TOUR 6

ISE

Today is an adventure in public transportation — ten boat, taxi, train and bus rides in six hours. Don't let the schedule intimidate you. It's more fun than a day at Blackpool Pleasure Beach. The views of the Izu Peninsula coastline, the bus trip out the Atsumi Peninsula and the ferry ride across the Mikawa-wan are breathtakingly scenic. This is also your first chance to meet some country people that don't see Gaijin every day. Have a go at conversation.

Suggested schedule	
8:00	Breakfast downstairs.
9:00	Walk over to the ferry boat pier, south of the hotel.
9:30	Blue and white ferry to Numazu.
9:45	Taxi from boat terminal to Numazu Eki.
10:53	Local to Mishima for the Shinkansen.
11:28	Kodama Super Express to Toyohashi.
12:40	Run, don't walk, out of the station and to the right for the Atsumi-sen train for Tahara.
12:45	Local train to Tahara.
13:20	Arrive Tahara and walk to bus stop, up the street to the traffic light and to the left about 15 feet.
13:37	Local bus to Irako-zaki.
14:30	Arrive Ferry Terminal and get ticket for 15:15 ferry to Toba.
15:15	Welcome to Ise! Taxi to Toba Eki (walk NE if you are so inclined). First available train to Kashikoshima, call for boat to come and take you across the lagoon to the Ishiyama So Minshuku.

Transport
Today's first leg on the ferry to Numazu follows the sheer coast of Izu. Walk down the beach from the minshuku to the sea wall south of town and buy a ticket for Numazu on the blue, white and red striped boat at 9:30. You want the small passenger boat, not the car ferry. The price, 2,200 yen (£10) per person, may seem a bit high, but the alternative is a 2,000 yen (£9) bus ride that takes twice as long.

Toi to Kashikoshima

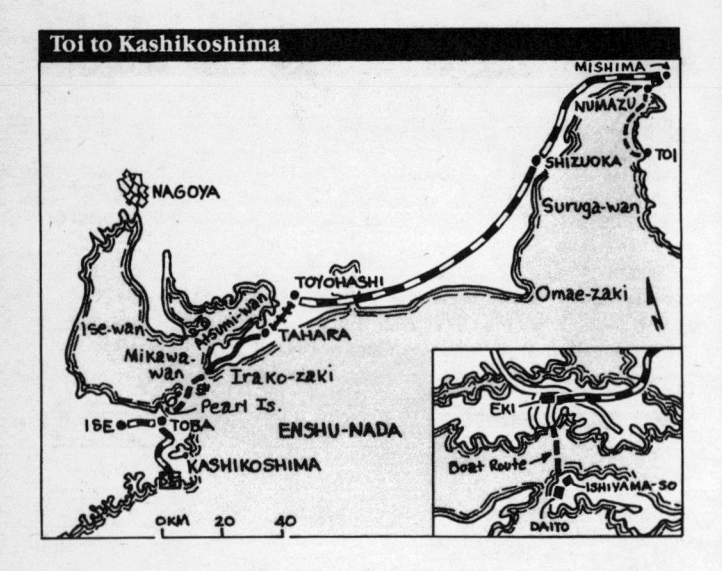

Take a taxi for the short ride from the ferry terminal to the Numazu station. Use your rail pass for the local hop to Mishima where you catch the Shinkansen Kodama for Toyohashi. The Kodama Super Express leaves Mishima at exactly 11:28.

Arriving in Toyohashi you have to move fast to make the local connection on the Atsumi-sen ('sen' means 'line'). Leave the station to your right and bear right along the station wall to another, smaller station immediately next door. If you hear the whistle blowing, forget the ticket; get on the trian and buy your ticket from the conductor. This train is not covered on your JR pass — 440 yen (£2), please.

You'll arrive in Tahara at 13:20 with plenty of time to walk up the street to the traffic light and turn left where the bus stop will be in front of you by the coke machines. The bakery on that corner also bears looking into.

The bus ride takes about an hour through rural Japan and offers tantalising glimpses of the Atsumi Bay on your right. The cost is 800 yen (£3.50).

At the ferry terminal you have time to get your 1,000 yen (£4.50) ticket. Make yourself a snack or get some soba at the stand inside. Notice the whale harpoon outside the terminal. (The last Japanese whaling expedition left for Antarctica in October of 1986, and Japan agreed to stop killing great whales at the end of the 1987 season thanks to extreme international pressure.) The Ise-Wan Ferry ('wan' means 'bay') takes an hour. You should be on the 3:15 ship.

From the Toba Ferry Terminal, catch a taxi again (no bus, at least not at the right time) to the Toba Eki. It's a 440 yen (£2) ride or a ten-minute walk. At the station go upstairs and buy a ticket for Kashikoshima, just 25 minutes away on a gorgeous train. Before leaving, call the minshuku, Ishiyama So. Ishiyama-san will meet you at the station when you arrive.

When you arrive at Kashikoshima, go downstairs and walk straight down to the waterfront where the inn's small boat awaits to take you across to the minshuku.

Accommodation
Ishiyama So: Kashikojima, Ago cho, Shima gun, Mie ken, Tel: 05995-2-1527. The people are nice, the accommodation clean and the view lovely. If you get the deluxe room for 8,000 yen (£36) (with meals) you will have your own toilet and bath, quite a luxury in a minshuku. Other rooms are available for about 5,500 yen (£25). Meals are downstairs and the view is at the front.

Daito: Same address, Tel: 05995-2-1136. Next door on the same islet is the Daito, much the same though the building itself has less character. Same prices, too.

TOUR 7

ISE – KYOTO

Today you'll see Japan's greatest national shrines. The Geku and the Naiku at Ise are the seat of Shintoism, Japan's own religion. On the way, you can also shop at one of the world's largest cultured pearl centres, Mikimoto's Pearl Island. Evening will find you in everyone's favourite Japanese city, Kyoto.

Suggested schedule	
7:30	Rise, eat and pack.
9:00	Leave for station.
9:30	Train for Ise-shi.
10:30	Bus from the No.1 stop for Naiku.
Midday	Tour the Naiku.
13:00	Lunch at Sandoh (2nd floor 2nd block from Eki).
14:00	Walk to Geku.
16:46	Tokyu (express) train to Kyoto, No.1 platform. Bus or taxi to pension or ryokan.

Transport

The Ishiyamas will boat you across the lagoon, and from there you retrace your steps of yesterday, passing Toba and going on to Ise-shi. If pearls interest you, see Mikimoto's Pearl Island — get off at Toba Eki and walk towards the ferry terminal — you can't miss it. Afterwards, simply catch the next available train to Ise-shi.

Ise Station has amply-sized lockers in which you can store your bags for the day. You can take a taxi or bus to the Naiku (Inner Shrine). See the Naiku first, as you will then be in town after seeing the Geku. If you are bussing it, the Naiku stop is to the right and in front of the station, just beneath the large cement torii (gate). It says number one, and it's the only one. The fare is about 350 yen (£1.50). If there are more than two in your party, the taxi will be as economical and quicker. After seeing the Naiku, return the way you came to the station or to the Geku.

After ranchi (lunch), walk up the street away from the station to the Geku, or Outer Shrine. See it at leisure.

The train connections to Kyoto are a little weak on this route so you have a whole afternoon before your leisurely ride to that city. Take your time at the shrines.

Arriving in Kyoto around 7.30 pm, you are better off taking a taxi to your nearby pension or ryokan. The taxi will take you up

Naiku

[Map showing: PARKING, MIKE-DEN, SHODEN, Koden-chi, TREASURIES, MAIN ENTRANCE, ANZAISHO, KAGURA-DEN, MAGATAKA, TSUCHINOMIYA SHRINE, KAZENOMIYA SHRINE, TAGONOMIYA SHRINE]

the hill with your bags, whereas the bus won't. Tell the driver, 'Shin Kiyo Mizu Miichi kudasai', and you will be taken to the right street. If you're staying at Kotomu, it is easily spotted on the dark street with its bright white sign in front. Teradaya is a hundred feet down the hill from Kotomu and to the left (north) in a little alley.

Sightseeing highlights

● **Pearl Island:** In Toba, this is the home of cultured pearls. Frequent pearl-diving displays by the Amas (lady divers) make this place worth a visit. They usually bring up only edible seaweed but it is interesting nonetheless. Skip the long-winded explanation of pearl culture unless the subject absolutely fascinates you. Note: if you want to buy pearls, the little shop by the boat landing in Kashikoshima has much better prices than Pearl Island. Haggle, but not too hard.

●●● **Naiku:** The sanctum sanctorum of the Shinto animistic religion. Devoted to Amaterasu-Omikami, the Sun Goddess, it is built of hinoki (cypress) and the architecture is pure Japanese with no Buddhist influence. The buildings are taken down and reconstructed every twenty years at great expense (it has been done for possibly the last time since the necessary skills are dying out). The unusual architectural style with the gables and gold decoration is called shimmei-zukkuri. On your way into the shrine get a pamphlet from the police box in front of the entrance. If it is very crowded, my hint of the day is to concentrate on the Kazahinomi-no-Miya and the Aramatsuri-no-Miya shrines which are off to the sides. The tours focus only on the main, central shrine.

●●● **Geku:** The Geku, or Outer Shrine, is the residence of the Imperial family when they come to Ise. It is devoted to Toyouke-Omikami, the goddess of agriculture. The shrine is architecturally similar to the Naiku, with some subtle differences in construction. The hills around the shrine are nice to walk and relax in.

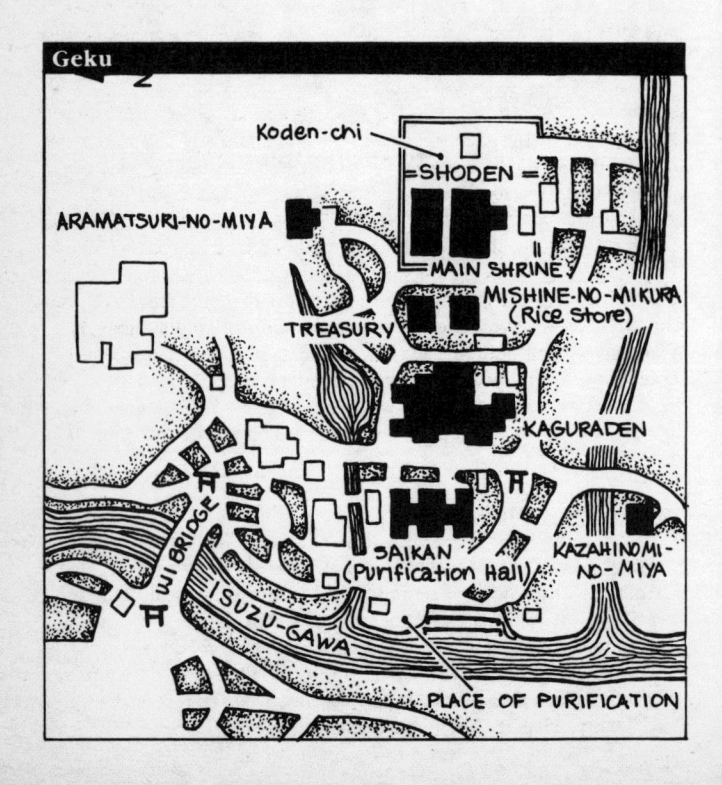

Note: photography is discouraged at both the Geku and the Naiku. You will see Japanese people taking pictures, but if you use your camera, be discreet about it. Better yet, buy slides.

Food: Naiku

Sandhu: Lunch can be had quite reasonably and edibly in this working-man's place. It's on the second floor, on the second block up from the railway station towards the Geku (southeast). Spaghetti Meato or Pizza Tosto are both decent. The lunch special is the Seto, working man's food. Say, 'Ran-chi seto kudasai'.

Pearl: A coffee shop with great coffee and o-shibori (hot or cold napkins depending on the season), near the station, if you have an hour to kill waiting for your train. Look for the Key Coffee sign out front, second block up from the station on the same side of the street as Sandhu.

Accommodation: Kyoto

Pension Kotomu: Gojobashi, Higashiyama-ku, Kiyomizu shin-miichi, Kyoto. Tel: 075-531-1848. The location is lovely, quiet and very convenient. Ask for the top floor room (there are only two). It has a nice balcony with a view of the city and Kiyomizu-tera. After three days this will feel like your neighbourhood. Staying at Kotomu you will be doing Kyoto as if you lived in a little apartment on the hillside, not a hotel room in the middle of town. The boss, Hirae-san, will take very good care of you. The price is fair, too, for Kyoto. 5,000 yen (£23) per person includes breakfast.

If you can't get into Kotomu go to **Ryokan Teradaya,** 583 Higashi Roku-chome, Gojobashi, Higshiyama-ku, Kyoto. Tel: 075-561-3821. Just down the street a short distance from Kotomu, this inexpensive ryokan caters to foreigners and locals alike. Pleasant, but without the view Kotomu has. The price is excellent at 4,000 yen (£18) with breakfast.

TOUR 8

KYOTO

Wake up and walk 100 yards to the beautiful Kiyomizu Temple to begin your tour of Kyoto's eastern hillsides — winding shop-filled alleys where a temple or shrine will greet you at every corner. Kyoto, the imperial capital of Japan for a thousand years, is overflowing with history and traditional architecture.

Suggested schedule

9:00	Kiyomizu Tera.
Morning	Walk across the hillside via Yasaka, Shoren-in and Chion-in to the Heian Shrine and possibly Ginkakuji.
	Lunch.
Afternoon	Nijo-Jo and whatever else you'd like to see.

Orientation

The Heart of Japan (Nihon no furusato) is how the Japanese think of this city. As the seat of government from 794 to 1868, its political fortunes waxed and waned but the essential spirit and culture remained, as did the Emperor. It is home to many of Japan's Buddhist sects, with over 2,000 temples and shrines. Everywhere you look, buildings and gardens evoke a strong feeling of antiquity and culture.

The city was laid out along the lines of Xian, the ancient capital of China, in a grid plan that makes it easy to get around. You can nearly always see the mountains that ring the city on three sides, so it is easy to keep your bearings.

The Kamo River flows along the eastern side of the city where many of the principal sights are located. Follow the river and you can't go too far wrong.

There are temples everywhere so it is impossible to say where a tour should begin. It is best to see the city in sections and don't attempt to see it all. See what you can, at a meditative pace. Don't skip here to see there. It is all worthwhile and enjoyable.

Maps and advice in English can be had from the TIC, located up the street in front of Kyoto Eki in the base of Kyoto Tower, the space-age-looking beast visible from anywhere in town. While there, be sure to pick up copies of the Kyoto and Nara Walking Tour Courses. These are very handy little brochures.

The JTB office is outside and to the right of the central exit to Kyoto Eki.

Scan your Walking Tour Course pamphlet with a map of the city alongside to get the lay of the land. Maps can be had, along with a great selection of English-language books, from Maruzen Books on Shijo-dori.

When your hillside stroll is over, take a taxi or bus to the other side of town for the walking tour of Kinkakuji and Ryoanji, or go and saunter around the grounds of Nijo-Jo. If your feet hurt too much for another walk, the Nijo castle is easier on them.

Trains, buses and the one-line subway are easy to use. The routes are marked on the city maps given out by the TIC.

Evening entertainment is found all over the city, ranging from the alleys of the Gion Quarter, lined with very expensive geisha houses, to the youthful, fun Kawaramachi district. The areas between Sanjo and Gojo-dori abound in fun and fascination. Wander at will, safe and sound.

Kyoto is nearly everyone's favourite city in Japan. See what you can and come back later for more.

Sightseeing highlights

●● **Kiyomizu Tera:** Built in 1633 by the Tokugawas, it is a National Treasure. The sanmon (entrance) is in classic Kyoto style Past this entrance is a three-storied pagoda, then the hondo (main hall). The hondo's terrace, supported by 139 wooden pillars, affords a fine view of the city. In front of the hall are the sandals of the giant who was defeated by the dwarf Issun-boshi. Past the terrace, the Otowa Falls are intended to be prayed under. Behind the hondo, be sure to see the Jishu Shrine. This colourful little shrine is devoted to Okininushi, the Japanese cupid. See if you can find the chief priest and speak to him. He is a Rotarian and a very gregarious fellow. The whole place is open during daylight hours. A fascinating sight is the monks, required by the order to beg for their food, working the neighbourhood early in the morning for breakfast.

● **Sannen Zaka:** Down the hill from the main entrance to Kiyomizu a little alley rambles across the hillside. Sannen-zaka has some of the loveliest handicraft you'll see anywhere in Japan at very reasonable prices. It's on the way to Yasaka and the rest of the walking tour.

●● **Kinkakuji:** At the time of writing, both Kinkakuji and Ginkakuji, the Silver and Gold Pavillions are closed to the public in a dispute with the city over the Historic City Preservation Tax, a local political dispute that unfortunately puts these major sights off limits. Check to see whether they've reopened by the time you arrive.

●● **Ryoanji:** Ryoanji is quintessential Zen. The fifteen rocks surrounded by white sand represent whatever you want them to

Kyoto

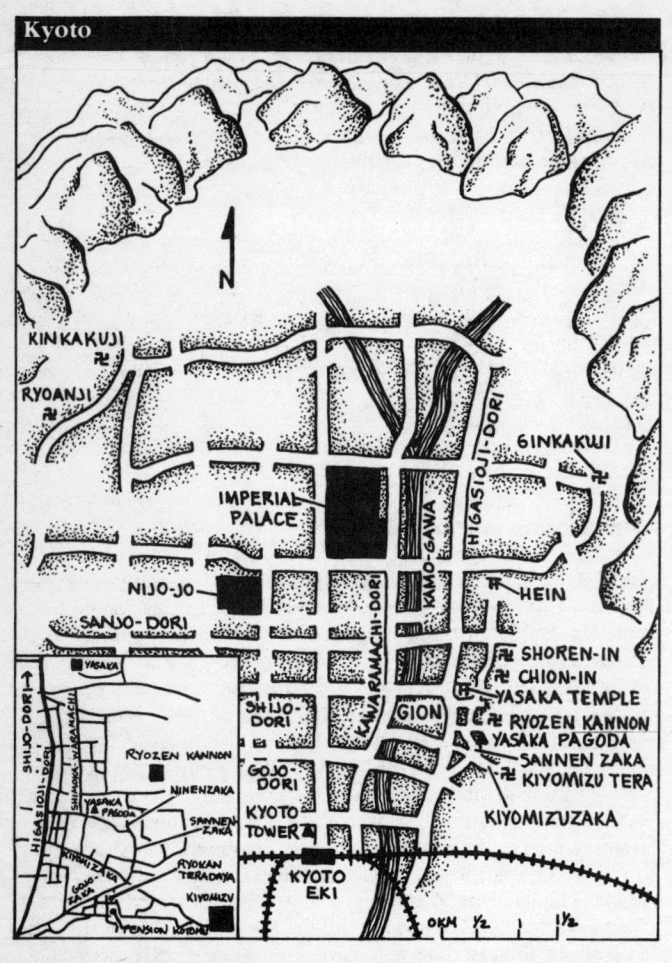

(Map of Kyoto showing locations including Kinkakuji, Ryoanji, Ginkakuji, Imperial Palace, Nijo-Jo, Sanjo-Dori, Heian, Shoren-in, Chion-in, Yasaka Temple, Ryozen Kannon, Yasaka Pagoda, Sannen Zaka, Kiyomizu Tera, Kiyomizuzaka, Gion, Kyoto Tower, Kyoto Eki, with streets Higashioji-Dori, Kawaramachi-Dori, Kamo-gawa, Shijo-Dori, Gojo-Dori, and inset showing Yasaka, Ryozen Kannon, Ninenzaka, Yasaka Pagoda, Sannen Zaka, Ryokan Teradaya, Kiyomizu, Pension Kyoto)

— cloud shrouded mountain tops or islands in the stream. It is the world's most famous rock garden.

● **Chion-in:** Home to the Jodo sect, it has a huge gate and Japan's largest bell. On your way across the hill, it is well worth a stop if only for the peace and quiet one may find here.

●●● **Nijo-Jo:** Built by Tokugawa Ieyasu in 1603, this castle was the residence of several Shoguns (supreme military rulers of united Japan). Tokugawa Ieyasu built it, and it bears testimony to his style and daring. Within, the Ninomaru Palace houses paintings by Kano Tanyu. The whole place is impressive and elegant. Take your time. The gardens and buildings are as good

as it gets in Kyoto, which is to say, in Japan. Closed on Mondays; admission is 450 yen (£2).
- **Gion Corner:** A touristy but fun spot to get a look at the 'clasic arts', such as Gagaku (ancient court music), bunraku (classic puppet plays) and dancing by geisha and maiko (apprentice geisha). It is in the centre of the Gion Quarter.

Food

Kyoto has its own food, known as Kyo-ryori or Kyoto cooking. Edo-ites (Tokyo) say that the southerners' food is too sweet and lacks salt or flavour. Perhaps true, but whatever it lacks in salt it makes up for with exquisite presentation and extraordinary delicacy. There are several types available: yusoku-ryori (concoctions for the Imperial court), shojin-ryori (Buddhist vegetarian food) and kaiseki-ryori (food prepared for the tea ceremony). All are available in many places of varying exclusivity. A commonly available version of kaiseki-ryori, the kyo-bento (a mouth-watering box lunch) is available in the basements of several large depaatos in town.

Kyoyamato Ryotei, right across the street from Ryozen Kannon, has a very Japanese-looking gate and gravel path leading into a garden. This is a wonderful but expensive kaiseki-ryori place. If you don't think you can stand the price tag on lunch (5,000 yen (£23)), at least have a look in the yard. If the old man is in the office in the entrance say, 'Chotto misete ii deska?' ('May I have a look?') and he will say (you hope), 'Hai, hai, hai, dozo' ('Yes, yes, go ahead'). The view of the Yasaka Pagoda from here is the best in town and the gardens are so typical of Kyoto that you'll remember them forever. Perhaps plan to eat there on your third day in town. (Call ahead for reservations; someone from your pension or ryokan can call for you.)

A lunch option if you want to try kyo-ryo at a reasonable price (3,000 yen (£14)) is **Mutsumi,** a lovely establishment, less fancy than Kyoyamato. The food is, all the same, very Kyoto. It is just in front of the east gate, the Torii of Yasuka Jinja. Reservations are a little less mandatory here but won't hurt (Tel: 525-0623).

Tohka Saikan: Chinese food. One of the few pre- WWII restaurants left in Kyoto, it is in a large building along the river on the west side of Shijo-dori bridge. The decor is like a set for an old Charlie Chan movie — pure Chinatown. Try their gyoza, fried pork dumplings, or the chien ti kua, tasty sugared fried sweet potatoes. The view over the river at night from the top floor dining room is excellent.

Torisei: Yakitori, neighbourhood style. Go down Kiyomizuzaka (Kiyomizu's main entrance) to Higashioji-dori and turn north (right). It is in the middle of the second block up. All kinds of chicken. Everything you can do to chicken (except chicken and biscuits). Say to the chef, 'Omakase shimasu' ('Please choose for me') and get a selection — all cooked, don't worry.

Nightlife

Make a point to see the Gion Quarter after dark. It will make you feel that you are in old Japan. If you're reading the book *The 47 Ronin*, you'll have a pretty good idea of what goes on behind those mysterious little doors. It is fun, but very expensive. If you can arrange for a Japanese businessman with an expense account to take you, fine. Otherwise, enjoy it from the outside.

The Kawaramachi area is more affordable. I've never been anywhere twice, in many nights of wandering this area, and I've always had fun. If you are unsure of what a place will cost, order a beer or cocktail and then ask for the bill.

The Kiyamachi area is loaded with hostess clubs. Stay away unless you feel like being fleeced. If you're offered little hors d'oeuvres the second you sit down, beware.

TOUR 9

KYOTO – NARA

A side trip to Nara today will round out your education in classical Japanese architecture and history. Nara, the original seat of government, today occupies a very important place in the nation's cultural consciousness, along with the Grand Shrine at Ise.

Suggested schedule	
8:52	JR line from Kyoto Eki to Nara. (You can save 26 minutes by taking the Kinki Nippon Line to Nara, but you have to buy a ticket.)
9:56	Arrive in Nara. See what you wish of Nara. Return when you like, even into the evening hours. Trains run every hour back to Kyoto, until 21:00.

Orientation

There is little left of the original Nara. Founded in 660 BC, the city has suffered vast swings of fortune's pendulum. It was the original seat of government where Jimmu Tenno sat as the first ruler of ancient Yamato, the Land of Great Peace. During the period up to 784 AD the area was the cultural centre of what is now Japan. Much was imported and assimilated from the T'ang Dynasty of China. This blending of Chinese and Japanese created the unique society and culture that lives on in 20th century Japan.

Nara has lost some of its charm to modern industrialisation, but the past is still vivid in many corners of the city, from back streets to the beauty of outlying Tenri. And Nara still has the Daibutsu, an enormous Buddha statue you won't forget.

Sightseeing highlights

●● **Kofukuji:** The Temple of the Establishing of Happiness is the home of the Hosso Sect. It originally belonged to the Fujiwara family (9th-11th centuries). It was razed in 1180 after the fighting monks of the temple backed a loser in a civil war. Rebuilt, then burned again in 1717, it has been faithfully reconstructed. The central feature, Nara's trademark, is the five story pagoda. The Chu-Kondo (central main hall) is worth visiting but the Nan-en-do is usually crowded; you might skip it if you can't get in the door. Nearby is the hall of Miroku Bosatsu, an image of the Buddha-to-be.

●●● **Kokuho-kan:** The Hall of National Treasures is filled with priceless relics from all over Nara, brought here to be preserved against pollution and fire — an unequalled treasure house.

●●● **Todaiji:** Great Eastern Temple, home of the Daibutsu, the Great Buddha. Founded in 745, it was to be the headquarters of all temples in Japan. It is the largest wooden building in the world, truly impressive. As you enter the Nandaimon, the great south gate, notice the Kongo-rikishi, lightning wielding devil gods. Inside you will come to the Daibutsuden, the Hall of the Great Buddha. Huge pillars support a ceiling hidden in twilight.

The Daibutsu: Dainichi-Nyorai, the Great Sun Buddha, sits in all his imposing bulk in the gloom of the huge hall. All other Buddhas and Bodhisattvas are beneath him in the hierarchy of Buddhism. Originally cast around 750, he has been redone in pieces due to fire damage. He is 71 feet tall and weighs 551 tons.

● **Kaidan-in:** West of the Daibutsu-den, this pine-enclosed Ordainment Platform is usually an island of quiet in the maelstrom of tourists swarming over the whole area. Built by the Emperor Shomu for the Chinese priest who converted him to Buddhism.

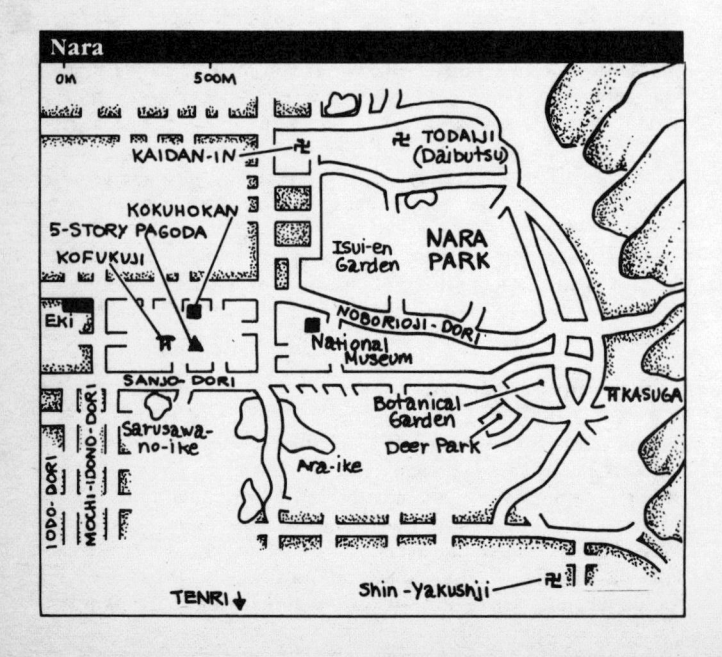

●● **Kasuga Shrine:** Founded in the early 700s by the Fujiwaras, it is noteworthy for its profusion of stone lanterns (some 3,000 of them). It is strikingly constructed of hand hewn timbers in the Kasugazukuri style, painted in vermillion and white.

●●● **Horyu-ji:** The oldest intact temple complex in Japan, it is reached by JR train from Nara Eki to Koriyama and then a 20-minute bus ride to the temple precincts. A prime example of the architecture of the Asuka Period, the home of the Shotoku Sect is one of the prime bastions of Japanese art, with works spanning the length and breadth of their history. The temple's kondo or main hall is the oldest wooden building in the world. The oldest pagoda in Japan is also on the grounds. 'Must-sees' are the Todaimon and the Yume-dono, the Hall of Dreams. An afternoon's worth of sightseeing.

●●●**Tenri:** A different sort of sect makes their home in the town of Tenri, on the main JR line out of Nara. They are the Tenri-kyo, a very outgoing sect. Somewhat neglected by mainstream tourists, they welcome visitors in a less commercial manner.

Itinerary options
There is so much to see in the Nara Basin that one day won't begin to be enough time. You might consider making time to stay here another day.

TOUR 10

HIMEJI AND KOTOHIRA

Ride the Shinkansen to Himeji, where you'll have time to visit one of Japan's best-preserved feudal castles, the Castle of the White Heron. In the afternoon, cross the Inland Sea to the island of Shikoku. Spend the night in the small town of Kotohira, site of Kompira Shrine. Feeling energetic? Want to stretch your legs after the train ride? Climb all 2,668 stairs to the Inner Shrine.

Suggested schedule	
8:15	After breakfast, check out and head for Kyoto Eki.
9:13	Shinkansen Hikari to Himeji.
10:09	Arrive in Himeji with two hours to see the Castle.
12:13	Shinkansen to Okayama.
12:47	Arrive Okayama with twenty minutes to make connection to JR Express to Uno.
13:46	Ferry from Uno to Takamatsu.
14:54	Arrive Takamatsu with a half hour to make the Ashizuri 7 to Kotohira.
Afternoon	Check into your hotel (ryokan). Afternoon free to see the Kompira Jinja.

Transport: Kyoto to Himeji

It's a short Bullet ride to Himeji where you have a couple of hours to see the castle. Arriving there you will have no trouble finding the Himeji-jo Castle as you can see it from the station. It's less than a kilometre up the street. There are lockers for your bags in the lobby of the station. If they are full you may be able to leave your bags under a table in the main ticket office. Ask nicely. As you really don't have that much time here, I recommend that you take a taxi for the short hop up the street to the castle. This way you will have time to see the castle thoroughly and still be able to stroll back to the station in time to catch your next ride.

Sightseeing highlight — Himeji

● ● ● **Shirasagi-jo, Castle of the White Heron:** Begun in 1333, it has been added onto by subsequent rulers. Toyotomi Hideyoshi was based here during his conquest of the Chugoku area. The castle reached its present size in 1624. Five storeys tall, built of rock, mortar and massive wooden beams it is a sterling example of feudal architecture — arguably the best castle in Japan. Nearly all the others have been destroyed by fire and reconstructed in modern times using cement rather than the huge wooden beams that give this castle its ancient, imposing feel. If you go in for castles at all (what real romantic doesn't?) you'll love this one. Catch it on a weekday when the crowds thin a bit and pretend you're the Lord of the Donjon himself. After seeing the castle, you should have time to walk down the boulevard and perhaps pick up lunch for the train ride.

Food: Himeji

There's a **Kentucky Fried Chicken** at the end of the arcade, one street over on the north side of the main road. Maybe you feel like something other than noodles and shrimp today (we all have our weak moments); the Colonel-san cooks tasty train food. Otherwise, lots of shops selling noodles, sushi and the like line the street leading to the castle in Himeji.

Transport: Himeji to Kotoshira

Leaving Himeji, get back on the Shinkansen and ride for a half hour to Okayama. There you get off the train and onto the express for Uno. A short ride will have you there, and all you have to do is walk off the train and go directly onto the ferry, which runs frequently. A half-hour cruise will have you on the smallest of the main islands, Shikoku.

When you arrive in Takamatsu, walk into the main train terminal and get on the Ashizuri Express for Kotohira. This is the last leg, I promise. You'll arrive in Kotohira at 16:16 with plenty of time to find your accommodation and still see the Shrine.

Sightseeing highlight — Kotohira

● ● ● **Kompira-Jinja:** Dedicated to Omononushi-no-mikoto, this delightful shrine was begun in the mid-1600s. Many sailors come here to pray for safe voyaging. The most noteworthy feature of this shrine is its profusion of stairs, some 2,668 of them. Climb as many as you possibly can — the Inner Shrine at the end is a wonderful place set in a grove of cedar and camphor trees. The road leading to the shrine is all stairs and pilgrim souvenir shops. Some of them have great stuff, such as a great carved wooden dragon — priced not to sell.

If you are not up to climbing all those stairs, despair not. There is a way out for the weak of knee. Litter bearers will carry you to the top in a little wicker contraption, for what I consider far too little money. There's a 180-pound weight limit.

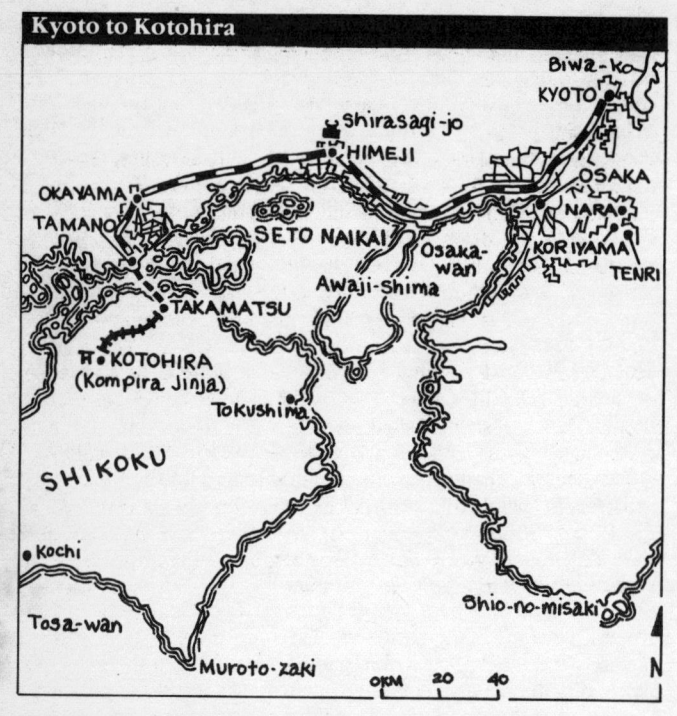

Accommodation

Kompira Prince Hotel: at Kagawa-ken, Nakatado-gun, Kotohira-cho, Esai 709, Tel: 0877-73-3051. This is a businessmen's hotel, close enough to walk to the shrine, although a taxi is not a bad idea. At 4,500 yen (£20) a night with breakfast (eastern or western), it is quite reasonable. You'll have western beds and a bath in the room.

Other lodging possibilities are two ryokan on the main road to the shrine, priced accordingly. Both are fairly nice; the more expensive of the two, the Kotohira Kadan, is worth the extra money. **Kotohira Kadan,** Kagawa-ken, Nakatado-gun, Kotohira-cho 1241-5, Tel: 08777-5-3232: the service is prompt and courteous to extremes. It is very traditional, and caters to the more affluent pilgrims that come to the Jija. Rooms from 10,000 yen (£45) up. The other ryokan is the **Kotohira Bizenya,** at Kagawa-ken, Nakatado-gun, Kotohira-cho 1241, Tel: 0877-75-3232. Rooms are 10,000 yen (£45).

There is a youth hostel, the **Kotohira Seinen no Ie,** on the hill behind the Kotohira Grand Hotel for 1,400 yen (£6.50) a night. It has a great location, the obasan (grandma) of the house is very nice, but it's none too clean. I once checked in and out in one hour. Maybe on a warmer night I'd have stayed: the view was very nice. Tel: 0877-73-3836.

Nightlife

Don't be out too late — you've got a lot more travelling ahead tomorrow. There isn't a lot to do in town after hours, anyway, but wander around and you'll find something.

An interesting drink to try here (or anywhere else, for that matter) is shochu lemon (pron: 'sho-choo remon'), a potent concoction of rice liquor and sugared lime juice. An interesting place to try one is **The Rumi Bar,** just down the hill from the Grand Hotel. The establishment is rather expensive. You see... ahem, how shall I put this ... there is company to be had. Sort of. It's a hostess bar, a charming provincial version of those hostess bars you should avoid in Tokyo and Kyoto. No real hanky-panky goes on. The girls will laugh at anything you say and maybe rub their knee against yours — but that's all. You're expected to buy them a beer or the like. The boss, a real gentleman, found me a room once when none were available in town (Wives and girlfriends may or may not enjoy this place; mine finds it hilarious.)

TOUR 11

MIYAJIMA

After travelling the length of northern Shikoku by train, board a high-speed boat to cruise across the most scenic neck of the Inland Sea, passing island after idyllic island en route to Hiroshima. Boat or train to the sacred island of Miyajima, where you'll spend the night.

Suggested schedule	
8:12	Local from Kotohira to Tadotsu.
8:27	Express from Tadotsu to Imabari.
10:59	Arrive Imabari and taxi (380 yen (£1.75)) to the Minato (ferry terminal).
	Lunch near the terminal, ticket (4,100 yen (£19)) in hand.
12:35	Boat to Hiroshima through the Inland Sea.
14:38	Arrive Hiroshima and get a ticket for:
15:15	Boat to Miyajima (Utsukushima), 1,080 yen (£5).
15:35	Arrive Miyajima and walk to ryokan.
Evening	Free to see the island.

Transport

Be at the station early to get a seat — the local is crowded with school kids on their way to another day. Try talking to them; they all want to try their English on you, even if it's only 'hello'.

The ride is short, and you have only a short wait for your express to Imabari. The train is on the next platform over. Ask anyway, 'Imabari wa nam ban desuka?' (Which number [platform] for Imabari?) If you can't count yet, have pen and paper in hand so they can write it for you. The scenery on the coastal sections of the rather long ride to Imabari is outstanding, and this is your main chance to see a chunk of Shikoku.

From Imabari Eki to the boat terminal is a short walk, but with luggage a taxi is recommended. It's a base price fare ride and the base in the sticks is lower than in the city — 380 yen (£1.75). You have an hour and a half, so it's a good time to get lunch and maybe wander around the busy little port by the terminal. Get your ticket before lunch on the off chance that the boat might be full. On weekdays you'll have no problem.

The ride through the Inland Sea (Seto Naikai) is superbly scenic. The boat windows are washed daily, so viewing and photography are unimpeded.

Arriving in Hiroshima you have two options: the easy, more costly one or the cheaper, more difficult one. From the Ferry Terminal at Hiroshima, a boat direct to Miyajima leaves shortly after you arrive (1,080 yen (£5)). For free (i.e. covered by your rail pass), you can take a train from near the terminal, through Hiroshima, to Miyajimaguchi where you can get a JR boat to Miyajima. The trip takes one and a half hours. I'd opt for more time on the island rather than on public transport. I don't want you to go broke; I just want you to see as much of the good stuff as possible.

Orientation

Miyajima, also known as Itsukushima, is ranked among the three most beautiful islands in the country. Until the reforms of the Mejii Period, no one was allowed to be born or to die on the island. Dogs were not allowed either. You're allowed to die there now if you want to, but you won't be buried there — and you still can't take your dog. To this day there is no cemetery on the island, and relatives of the dead must undergo rites of purification after funerals before they may return home. A favourite of the great founder priest Kobo-daishi, Miyajima is still revered today as a pure beautiful island.

Sightseeing highlights

● The first sight that greets you upon arrival on Miyajima is a line of shops selling the usual snacks and souvenirs. The little automated bean cake making machines are interesting, even if the product they turn out isn't. Perhaps you'll like those sugary, beaney, brown confections, but I doubt it. Try just one before you buy a box.

●● **Torii:** The great red gate out in the water (or in the mud, depending on the tide), one of the most photographed objects in Japan, is Japan's largest torii, 53 feet tall. It was erected in 1875 and is still in good shape today. Lovely at night.

●● **Itsukushima Shrine:** Dedicated to the daughters of the Wind God, Susano. First built in 811, it has since been reconstructed many times. It is built in classic Shinto fashion with the many buildings separated by decking over the water. At high tide, the buildings appear to be floating on the water, as does the Torii, which is in line with the shrine. Dances are performed in the shrine for a fee, but the crowds make the viewing best from outside.

●● **Treasury:** A modern fire and earthquake proof building, it is not much to look at, but within are 130 National Treasures.

● **Hall of a Thousand Mats:** Constructed in 1587 by Toyotomi Hideyoshi, one of medieval Japan's most powerful military leaders, and dedicated to his memory, the hall is said to have been built from the wood of a single camphor tree. There are really only about 450 mats, but it is impressive all the same.

Accommodation
Ask the Tokyo Minshuku Centre for help in finding reasonably priced accommodation on Miyajima. One possibility is **Kamefuku,** 849 Miyajimacho, Saeki-gun, Tel: (08294) 4-2111. 15,000 to 20,000 yen (£68 to £91) includes two meals.

If Miyajima is too expensive, or no lodging is to be found, stay the night in Hiroshima and commute to Miyajima for the day. It's less than an hour's travel each way, so this poses no great problem. Try exploring in the outskirts of Hiroshima — there's something to see in every small town between Miyajima and Hiroshima. Be adventurous.

TOUR 12

MIYAJIMA

A day free to relax and enjoy this splendid little island. Miyajima, particularly on a weekday in fine weather, is an easy place to spend a day. See the main sights you missed yesterday. Ride the ropeway or better yet climb through Momijidani to the top of Mt Misen. Or go on an all-day walk around the island. Early morning and the evening are the best times to see the main sights unmolested by crowds. The day is yours to do as much or as little as you please.

Suggested schedule
Forget about your itinerary. You're on vacation!

Sightseeing highlights
●●● The view from the top of **Mt Misen** commands a sweeping vista of the Seto Naikai. The Gumonji-do Temple at the top is a particularly fine viewing spot. Best in the evening when the crowds have thinned. The walk up from the bottom through the Momijidani or Maple Valley is breathtaking, particularly in the spring and autumn. Tea houses in the valley make for a nice afternoon refreshment interlude. Just west of Momijidani is the ropeway to the top (800 yen (£3.50)). Why not ride it up, then walk back down?

●●● **Walk around the island.** An all day proposition, you can swim on seven lovely beaches and call it a pilgrimage. A picnic lunch (read 'o-bento') from your ryokan or a restaurant is mandatory.

Itinerary options
If you crave big city action, it's easy enough to go into Hiroshima for the afternoon and evening. Transport is described in Tour 13. You could see Peace Park and the Shukkeien Gardens today and sleep in tomorrow or head south earlier.

TOUR 13

HIROSHIMA – TRAVEL TO KYUSHU

Return to Hiroshima for a visit to Peace Park to see the place where nuclear war actually happened. Then head for Kyushu, the southernmost major island of Japan. The Bullet train makes quick work of a long trip. Stay sober on the train — you'll be driving when you arrive.

Suggested schedule	
8:00	Leave Miyajima via JR Ferry.
9:00	JR local to Hiroshima Eki.
9:25	Morning free to see Peace Park and a little of Hiroshima.
12:25	Shinkansen Kodama for Hakata.
14:15	Arrive in Hakata and head for subway to Karatsu.
16:00	Arrive in Karatsu and rent a car. Drive to Yobuko or Hatomisaki, about an hour's leisurely trip.

Transport: Miyajima to Hiroshima

Catch a ferry to the mainland around eight so as to make a connection to Hiroshima on the trains, which are crowded even though they run often early on. The JR ferry is in the first building in the ferry complex. Wave your rail pass at the ticket window and you'll know immediately if you have the right line. No ticket is necessary on JR locals — just your rail pass.

Once on the mainland at Miyajimaguchi, walk outside the ferry terminal and up the way to the west, across a rather large street to the big terminal. It's not the tiny station just outside the ferry terminal; that's a local that takes twice as long and costs real money. Go to the one that looks like a train station.

Ride the first available local to Hiroshima. The platform is across the tracks. Ask anyway. 'Hiroshima wa nam ban desuka?' ('What number (platform) for Hiroshima?') The agent will probably respond, 'Ni ban desu' ('Number two').

Arriving in Hiroshima about twenty-five minutes later, head for the lockers at the extreme south end of the station on east side. They are rather well hidden behind a coffee shop in the corner. Stow your gear and head for Peace Park (Heiwa Koen) by taxi or bus. The taxi is around 800 yen (£3.50), the bus 200 yen (90p). The bus stand is on the eastern side of the station.

Sightseeing highlights
● ● ● **Peace Park:** At 8:15 am, 6 August 1945 an atom bomb was detonated on the civilian target of Hiroshima. The Chamber of Commerce stood at the epicentre. What is left of it is now called the Atom Dome. It and the rest of the park are very sobering indeed. The Peace Memorial Museum is full of grisly photographs and mementoes of the blast. No fun, but something that everyone should see, including the leaders of a few countries I could mention.

The Monument to the Victims of the Atomic Bomb is an arch through which you can see the Atom Dome. On it is written, 'Rest in peace, for this error shall not be repeated.' This is very much the attitude of the people of Hiroshima. They don't want it to happen again — to anyone.

Transport to Karatsu, then to Yobuko or Hatomizaki
Around eleven o'clock you need to head back to the station to catch a train for Hakata on the island of Kyushu. Before you leave, you might wander down into the underground shopping arcade to get a bite to eat on the train. The bakeries down there sell very good sandwiches.

If you can get on a Bullet to Hakata around noon, do so. If not, the 12:25 will do fine. Platform 11 for your train (check this — schedules change).

Ride the train for an hour and three quarters or until it doesn't go any further and you'll be at Hakata, Fukuoka City, the end of the line. Get off and head down to the well-marked subway. Buy a 200 yen (90p) ticket and get on a train for Karatsu. The 200 yen is for the inner-city underground portion of the trip; your rail pass covers the rest.

Ride until you reach Karatsu, again the end of the line. It will take another hour and three quarters.

Had enough trains yet? If so, you'll be glad to rent a car in Karatsu. Otherwise, buses are also available to Yobuko and Hatomizaki. They are in front of the station, and there's an information booth in the station lobby.

If you are driving, take it easy at first. Read the section on driving in the front of this book before you take off. Keep to the coastal route and you can't go wrong. Getting out of town is the only hard part. If you pass a McDonald's, you're going the wrong way. Find out whether a Japanese 'Biggu Makku' tastes the same as back home, have some great french fries and be on your way in the opposite direction.

It's a half hour or so drive along the coast to Yobuko, a quaint little fishing town.

Hiroshima: Peace Park

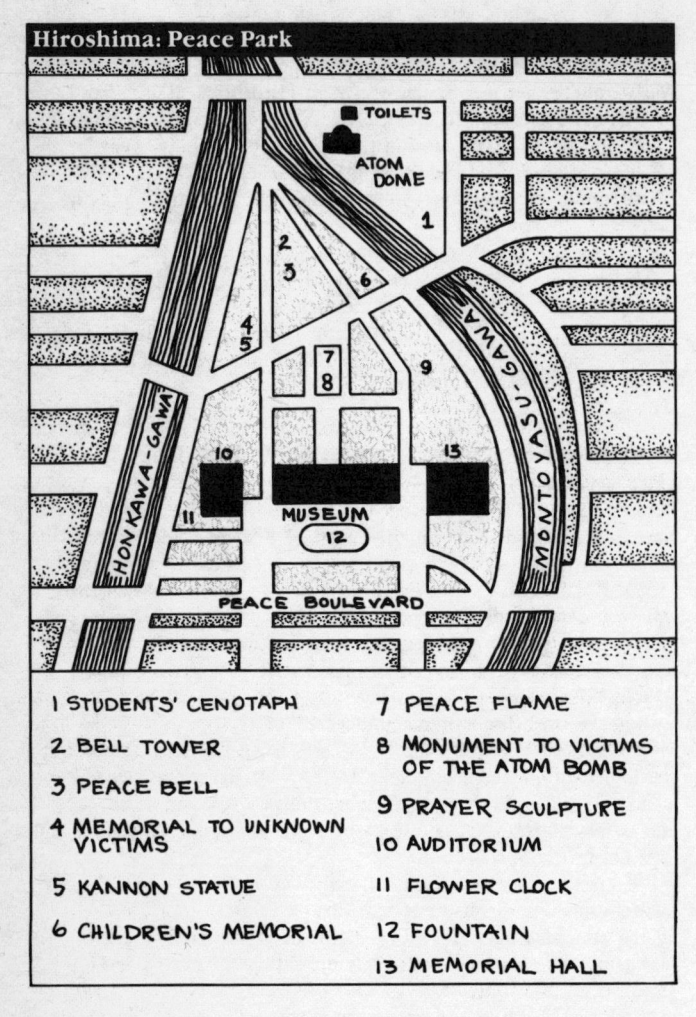

1. STUDENTS' CENOTAPH
2. BELL TOWER
3. PEACE BELL
4. MEMORIAL TO UNKNOWN VICTIMS
5. KANNON STATUE
6. CHILDREN'S MEMORIAL
7. PEACE FLAME
8. MONUMENT TO VICTIMS OF THE ATOM BOMB
9. PRAYER SCULPTURE
10. AUDITORIUM
11. FLOWER CLOCK
12. FOUNTAIN
13. MEMORIAL HALL

Car hire

Hiring a car will make this a lovely wandering, exploring segment of your trip. I strongly recommend that you plan to have 19,000 yen (£85) set aside for this or a credit card you can worry about when you get home. Buses can take you where you're going, but it's fun to wander around this area and hard to get too lost. If you do decide to rent a car, Eki Rent-A-Car is just outside the station in a little booth in the car park. The fellows don't speak English, but if you show up with an International Drivers

Licence (purchased from the AA at home), your regular licence, preferably a credit card, and money in hand, you should have no trouble. Get a map and say 'Yoboku wa doko desuka?' ('Where is Yoboku?'), and they'll draw a line for you. ('Map' is 'cheezu' in Japanese, by the way. 'Cheezu' also means 'cheese' but that's irrelevant unless you really need a sandwich right now.) A two day rental for a car like a Toyota Tercel is 19,000 yen (£85) including insurance (hoken).

Accommodation

Decide whether you want a real ryokan tonight. The price is a little bit higher, but the service is worth it and this might be a good place to splash out on a 'real' Japanese inn. If expense is not a major concern, I suggest you stay one night at the Tsuruya Ryokan in Yobuko and one night at the Sea Side Pension on the cape. A more affordable option is to spend both nights at the Sea Side Pension. If the car hire cramps your budget, rather than forego it and take the bus you could economise by staying at the National Citizens' Hotel in Hatomizaki.

Tsuruya Ryokan is in Yobuko, right on the water, and all rooms overlook the bay. You can toss rice crackers out of the window to the fish. The service is much better than you usually get for the price, 8,000 yen (£36) per person with two great meals. The place is a little on the old side but very nice. It is on a narrow little street on the opposite side of the bay from where you come into town on Highway 204. Keep going until you see a little bridge on your right, cross it, and bear right along the water. Go past a large grocery shop and keep going down the lane. The ryokan has a little two-car car park on the opposite side of the street. Tel: 9558-2-3414.

Sea Side Pension, Saga ken, Higashi Matsubara gun, Chinzei cho, Hado, 748-2 Tel: 09558-2-1288. A really nice psuedo-European pension for 6,500 yen (£30) per person, beautifully sited on a hill overlooking the whole cape area — look for the new white building. Large amounts of western style food and beds (tatami, Japanese-style rooms are also available if you can't stand the thought of sleeping on a bed). Run by the Kubashima family. The views are great from most rooms.

The Hatomizaki **National Citizens' Hotel** (Kokuminsha) at Saga ken, Matsubara gun, Chinzei cho, Hado 1082, Tel: 09558-2-1511, is out on the cape. The location is lovely and the price is right, even if the place resembles a youth hostel (both private rooms and dormitory). The food is not so hot, and unless you're driving you're stuck here. I could think of worse places to be stuck, though. Around 3,000 yen (£13.50).

Itinerary options
You are not seeing what most Gaijin see of Kyushu. The normal tour would include Nagasaki, a lovely city with a lot of Dutch influence, and at least one or two hot spring resorts such as Beppu or Ibusuki. If you have the time, any of these would make a pleasant two-day side trip.

TOUR 14

YOBUKO TOWN – HATOMIZAKI

Drive around the peninsula and explore. The coastline here is reminiscent of the fjords of Scandinavia — tiny narrow bays and inlets, with jewel-like villages nestled down in the bottoms. Today is casual. If you wake up early enough, see the morning market in Yobuko. If you feel you need to sleep late, go ahead and sleep. The day is yours.

Suggested schedule	
Morning	Market or Asa iichi in Yobuko Town. See the fascinating boats and activity on the wharf. Drive to the Underwater Observatory Tower on Cape Hatomizaki.
Afternoon	Free to beachcomb or drive down the coast for a picnic.

Transport

Driving, it's easy to get lost. Fortunately, you have ocean on one side and mountains on the other. Stick to the coastal areas and keep an eye on your compass. I don't read Kanji any better than you do, and I've never been lost for long around here. Most roads lead back to where you began, in Karatsu, less than an hour away.

Wander down along the coastline towards Hatomizaki and the Underwater Observatory. Bear right each time you have a choice of major roads and you'll find it.

Try some small roads and even a dirt road or two if you are so inclined. Explore with your wheels. A car gives you an unaccustomed freedom that you will soon love.

If you do get lost, as a last resort call the Travel Phone (reverse charges) for help. Look in the back of this book for phone numbers, or just dial O and say 'TIC collect call' ("Tee-aye-she, corecto-coru") in your best unaccented Japanese. Explain your situation to the person on the line, and they can translate to some helpful bystander you have managed to snag.

Sightseeing highlights

● **Asa-ichi:** The Yobuko morning market is on the street just behind the main road along the waterfront. Vegetables and the night's catch. It starts around 7:00 am. If you spent the night in Yobuko, you probably heard the boats going out at three in the morning.

Hatomizaki

●● **Omishima Jinja:** My secret picnic spot in Kariya Wan. As you drive south, keep to the coast past the atomic power plant. Turn down promising roads until you come to a beautiful bay with a huge rounded rock formation and a little fishing village nearby. At the south end of town you'll find a small island surrounded by mud flats with a sea wall around it. Behind a large office building, a path leads up to Omishima Jinja, a wonderful, derelict little Shinto shrine. Over the hill is a sea wall with a back rest and a ship wreck to look at while you eat. (These directions are vague on purpose — after all, it's a secret. If you find it, please keep it clean. Thanks.)

●● **Hatomizaki Undersea Observatory:** A tower lets you go down below the water level to view the thousands of fish that swarm along the coast. They swarm in the water, making for a spectacular number of little fish.

Food

As you leave Yobuko, there's a large grocery shop on the south side of the road (away from the water), on the same street as the Tsuruya Ryokan. A good place to pick up picnic supplies, they have good bread, canned tuna and handy two-sandwich squeeze bottles of mayonnaise, lemon and cucumber. Sounds like a tuna fish sandoichi to me. They also have peanut butter and Japanese salamis.

TOUR 15

HATOMIZAKI – KYOTO

Suggested schedule	
8:30	Check out and hit the road to Karatsu.
10:12	Leave Karatsu by local for Hakata.
11:25	Arrive in Hakata and connect to:
12:02	Shinkansen for Kyoto.
16:33	Arrive at Kyoto Eki.
	Afternoon and evening on the loose in Kyoto again.

Transport

Try to be on the road by 8:30 so you'll have a little buffer time in case of a wrong turn. A hint if you're driving — turn right out of the entrance road to the pension and the citizens' hotel. Head north on 204 toward Karatsu. Stay with the coast and the main road all the way to town. In Karatsu again, if you see McDonalds you have gone one street too far. Go around the block McD's is on, back one street, and turn left. You can see the station at the end of the street. Go past the car park where the car rental agency is and turn right. Cross the little bridge; to the left you'll see a petrol station. Fill up and get the attendant to stamp the little white piece of paper the rent-a-car people gave you at the beginning. It should cost about 1,600 yen (£7.25) if you drove quite a bit. Back at the rental stand, hand over the keys and the folder. You're done.

Board the 10:12 train for Hakata and stay on it to the end of the line. You have a half hour there before your 12:02 departure. There's a bakery for sandoichis but the food on this train is really tasty. ('What,' you say, 'edible train food?' Yes it's true. The food on this run, furnished by the Miyako Hotel Kyoto, measures up to their fine reputation.) I highly recommend the tonkatsu set, a really good box lunch.

Ride that train all the way to Kyoto.

In Kyoto you have the late afternoon to check back into your hotel and stroll a bit before dinner. I leave the itinerary up to you. You're an old hand here now, right?

TOUR 16

TRAVEL TO HAKUI

Today you're off to the west coast — lovely to look at and, unlike the east coast, very sparsely populated. Agriculture, rather than industry, occupies most people here. In Kanazawa, stroll through one of Japan's most beautiful formal gardens. Overnight in the small town of Hakui, in a lovely traditional beachfront neighbourhood.

Suggested schedule	
	Up early and be at Kyoto Eki for:
9:34	Kodama Express for Maibara.
9:55	Arrive in Maibara and change for:
10:23	Koetsu Tokyu for Kanazawa, Platform 7, but check anyway.
12:07	Arrive in Kanazawa.
	Free until three to see the Gardens.
15:03	Local JNR to Hakui.
	Taxi to your minshuku. Remainder of the afternoon free for the sights.

Transport: Kyoto to Kanzawa

It's a short ride to Maibara on the Kodama Express. Change there to a normal Express (Koetsu Tokyu) for Kanazawa.

Sightseeing highlights — Kanazawa

● ● **Kenroku-en:** This is one of the three most beautiful gardens in Japan. It was created in sections meant to represent various aesthetic qualities: coolness, dignity, festivity, artistic form, spaciousness and scenic harmony. Laid out in 1837 for the Maeda family, it has everything a proper Japanese garden should have — grace, character, variety and tranquillity.

A bus to the park leaves from the number 10 or 11 stop in front of the Kanazawa train station (150 yen (70p) for a short ride). You'll probably be happy for at least an hour and a half there but if you get tired you'll find enough to keep an inveterate shopper happy in the Korinbo and Kitamachi market areas, both near enough to the station to make a quick taxi ride feasible.

Food (Kanazawa)

At the station in Kanazawa they sell the best o-bentos you ever had. Kani-ben is a smoked salmon on rice, an ebi-ben is shrimp and vegetables on seasoned rice and there are others. Take one on a picnic with you to the gardens.

Transport: Kanzawa to Hakui

In Kanazawa, check the schedule for your last ride of the day, an hour on the local train to Hakui.

Upon arrival, take a taxi to your minshuku, especially if you are staying at Tarosuke. It is a bit hard to find, but all the locals know the place.

Check in, then have a walk. If daylight allows walk down the beach to the cement torii, then turn up the hill to the shrine.

Hakui

The scenery isn't astonishing and when you get to the station you may wonder why you are here. It really is a charming little town with a lovely set of shrines and temples. The people here don't see a lot of Gaijin, as most group tours head up to the better-known areas of the Noto Hanto such as Wajima and Nanao.

If it's warm out, the sea is right in front of the minshuku for swimming. Even if it's not, it's great for beachcombing.

Sightseeing highlights — Hakui

●● **Keta Taisha Shrine:** This small shrine has a sacred, virgin woods that the Emperor is very fond of. The Chief Priest, Mitsui-san is a famous calligrapher as well as a most agreeable and helpful gentleman. Search him out if you can and say hello. At the Shrine office you can get an English history of the shrine.

●● **Myojoji Temple:** Down the road, a short bus ride from Keta Taisha or take the bus from the stop behind the minshuku. The temple belongs to the Niichiren Buddhist Sect, a relatively new group. About twenty years old, the five-storey pagoda exemplifies new Buddhist architecture.

Accommodation

Tarosuke: Located near the shrines in one of the nicest neighbourhoods you will have the pleasure to see on this trip. Run by an obaa-san (grandmother) and her daughter. Obaa-san is a real sweetheart who will laugh with and at you. She is 80 years old, and I hope has lots more left to enjoy.
Tel: 1762-2-0616.

Food: Hakui

In Hakui you can eat in at the minshuku or walk out for a bite. If you're at Tarosuke, you have to walk some way down the road to a restaurant near the freeway (east) to find anything. A place called **Mitakeya** has good reasonably priced food.

TOUR 17

TRAVEL TO SADO ISLAND

Today is a long travel day. The sights en route will more than make up for your pains. This scenery along this part of the west coast will impress you, the food in Niigata will tantalise your palate, and the Island of Sado will totally captivate you.

Suggested schedule	
7:00	Breakfast. Get packed and paid up, leave your bags at minshuku.
8:00	Walk to Keta Shrine or take the bus to Myojoji.
10:15	Retrieve your luggage and be at station for:
10:37	Local to Kanazawa.
11:55	Hokuetsu Express for Niigata.
15:42	Arrive in Niigata, dinner, then taxi or bus to the ferry terminal for:
18:50	Ferry to Ryotsu-shi on Sado Island.
21:20	Arrive (finally) on Sado. Bed probably sounds about right.

Transport: Hakui to Niigata

Ask someone at the minshuku to call a taxi to pick you up at 9:30. Say 'Takushi kudasai, ku ji han goro' ('Could I have a cab around 9:30, please?') If you saw the Keta Taisha Shrine yesterday, but missed Myojoji, take a bus from the Taki bus stop behind the minshuku to Myojoji. It is only a 3 km ride.

Back at Tarosuke, tell the cabbie, 'Eki kudasai,' to get back to the station. Catch the 10:37 local to Kanazawa. There will generally be no food on the train to Niigata until about halfway through the ride, when excellent o-bentos are brought on board. There are some shops in the basement of the Kanazawa station, and good o-bentos are available in the station itself.

From Kanazawa, ride to Niigata on the 11:55 express. The train ride north along the coast is scenic in the extreme: Snow-capped mountains of Chubu Sangaku National Park on the right and the Sea of Japan on the left. One could do worse for an afternoon train ride. Arriving at Niigata, get your tickets for the ferry boat. The **Sado Kiisen Agency** (travel agents), in a little booth outside in the front of the terminal, can take care of all your needs while on the island.

Food: Niigata

When you arrive in Niigata, you'll have a couple of hours on

your hands before your 18:50 ferry to Sado. I wouldn't call
Niigata a really fantastic town to kill time in, but it has a couple
of redeeming restaurants.

Jukoan is popular with the upward movers of Niigata. Run by
a husband and wife team named Takegahara, this kushiyaki place
will delight you with the range of flavours presented, many of
them new to the western palate. It's not exactly cheap, but it is
so good that you won't fret too much over two or three thousand
yen apiece for a great meal. If the mistress is in, give her my
regards and help her practise her English. You'll find Jukoan on
Furuimachi-dori, a large shopping-arcade street up the main road
from the station about 1½ kilometres. Take a bus up that way
until you see an arcade off on either side, then go north about
two blocks. Jukoan, on the left, has a grey frosted glass door. Sit
at the counter even if you have to wait a bit.

Your other option is to go to **Kotobukiya** for some fantastic
Chinese food. Great gyoza (pork dumplings), delicious ramen
soup — extremely piquant and filling, very reasonably priced.
Kotobukiya is up the street from Jukoan in a little alley. Find
Jukoan and ask for directions, both places are in the family.

Transport: Niigata to Sado Island
After dinner in Niigata, take a bus to the ferry terminal. The bus
depot is right in front of the station on the south side. The ride
is short, but if you don't mind 800 yen (£3.50) the taxi is easier
after dinner. The ferry terminal is self-explanatory.

A pleasant (weather permitting) cruise will take you to Ryotsu
City, where you will be met (if they're expecting you) by
someone from the Sado Seaside. If not, take a taxi to your
lodgings, then to bed with you.

Accommodation
Sado Seaside Hotel, 80, Sumiyoshi, Ryotsu shi, Niigata ken,
Tel: 02592-7-7211, 4,500 to 9,000 yen (£20 to £40). The hotel
has a hot-spring fed tub that you might enjoy if the day hasn't
been altogether too long. The beach is nearby but you won't be
needing it unless you are an early riser. In Aikawa a very nice
ryokan is the **Yamaki Hotel** 361, Kabuse, Aikawa-machi,
Sadogun 952-15. More expensive (9,000 yen (£40)) and also
perhaps hard to find late at night. Or in Niigata, **Niigata Onoya
Ryokan,** 981, Furuimachi-dori, Rokuban-cho, Niigata Shi 951.

TOUR 18

SADO

Relax and drive yourself around an island so exotic looking, you'll think you've been transported into an ancient oriental landscape painting. You can't get lost — there's only one road.

Suggested schedule	
Daytime	Sleep as late as you please (but not past nine) Pick up your rent-a-car and head out for: Aikawa — you should arrive around noon. See the mines. Continue around Sado until you reach the northern cape and the village of Negai. Check into the San Kei Kan.
Evening	Walk, swim and enjoy.

Transport

First thing, get yourself organised with a car. Read the section on driving if you haven't already. A 24 hour rental period should cost from 9,500 to 25,000 yen (£43 to £114) depending on how glorious a chariot you choose. The cheap model should be fine.

Head out of town for Aikawa. Get the rent-a-car man to put you on the right road towards Aikawa. Say 'Aikawa wa dochira no ho desuka?' ('Which way is Aikawa?') and he should point out the direction at least. Go east over the biggest mountain you can find or across the narrow neck of the island and you should do fine.

Don't linger too long in the mines, because the drive north around the west coast is the main attraction today. You can't miss it as there is only one road and one coastline.

Go north around the island until you get to what is obviously the northern cape, about a two hour drive if you don't hurry too much. This is Hajikizaki, the northern end of nowhere on Sado. Go around the cape until you see a resthouse/hostel on the right hand side of the road. Just past there about a half a kilometre on the left, a narrow road winds down the hill to the fishing village of Negai. The San Kei Kan Minshuku is the first in the line of inns on the beach.

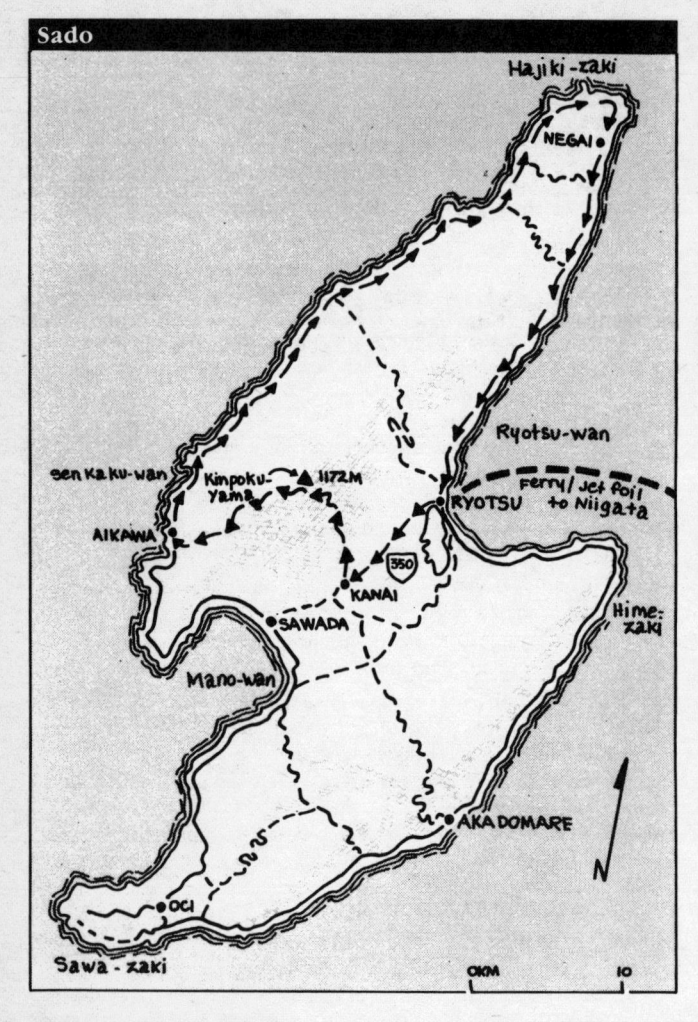

Sightseeing highlights

● ● ● **The scenery.** As you drive around the island, sheer, plunging cliffs, dive into the Sea of Japan. Offshore, tiny islets sport gnarled and twisted pines like ancient scroll paintings. Off to the sides of the main road, dirt roads and paths beckon to the adventurous. It's a wonderful drive.

● ● **Aikawa** is the sight of one of the oldest gold mines in the country. It's done up like an amusement park, but tasteful. The shafts are very interesting especially in light of the fact that they were built without machinery. The life size animated characters down in the hole would do Disney proud — very Pirates-of-the-Caribbean-ish.

●●● **Crystalline waters.** If the weather is warm, you might consider getting a cheap diving mask from one of the shops in Negai. The water is gorgeous. The beach is rock but it makes for marvellous swimming all the same.

●● **The path south from Negai.** Walking down the path from your lodgings you will come to grotesque rock formations and small shrines in tiny cliff-side grottoes. Fascinating.

Car hire
In Ryotsu-shi, contact the Sado Kiisen (Agency for Sado Tourism), Tel: 02592-7-5195.

Accommodation
San Kei Kan: Ryotsu shi, Negai 260, San Kei Kan, Tel: 02592-6-2440. The Kitazawa family runs this archetypal beach minshuku and a more hospitable group you won't meet anywhere. Ojii-san (grandpa) is the salt of the earth. It's worth learning Japanese just to speak with him. His grandson, Ryusan, is a friend of mine. If you're lucky and he's not too busy with his school work, maybe he'll show you around a little bit. He is very bashful but toys and fireworks can help break the ice.

TOUR 19

SADO TO BANDAI

Today you'll travel into the breathtaking mountains of central Honshu. The day starts with a drive down the stunning coast of eastern Sado, followed by a ride on one of the world's fastest boats, then a trip into the 'Japanese Alps' on a rustic diesel train.

Suggested schedule	
9:00	Leave Negai south to Ryotsu.
11:00	Jet-foil from Sado to Niigata.
12:00	Arrive in Niigata, bus or taxi to Niigata Eki.
13:35	Local for Inawashiro.
17:39	Arrive in Inawashiro.
18:10	Bus to Bandai Kogen.

Transport: Sado to Niigata

Allow an hour and a half for the drive down the coast to Ryotsu. When you drop the car off, the rent-a-car people will take you back to the terminal for your jet-foil ride back to the mainland. Built by Boeing Aircraft, the jet-foil is one fast boat (50 mph).

In the row of shops behind the ferry terminal in Ryotsu-shi, you'll find beautiful Sado handicrafts — wickerwork and interesting curios — for sale at very reasonable prices, especially if you haggle.

Food: Niigata

McDonalds (in case you've weakened by now) is a three-minute walk from the terminal in Niigata. Walk a couple of hundred yards west up the main road and turn left. Keep an eye out for the bus terminal and the Isetan department store. By the way, Isetan runs the best department stores around.

Transport: Niigata to Ura-bandai

When you arrive in Niigata, a bus will be waiting outside to take you to the train station. Get to the terminal and organise some lunch for the ride or eat here. The train to Inawashiro is a local all the way. The seats aren't the greatest, but the scenery is enough to keep your mind off your derriere and out of the window.

You'll be winding up the Agano River most of the way to Aizu-Wakamatsu, passing through a dozen hot spring towns that aren't

Niigata to Chuzenji

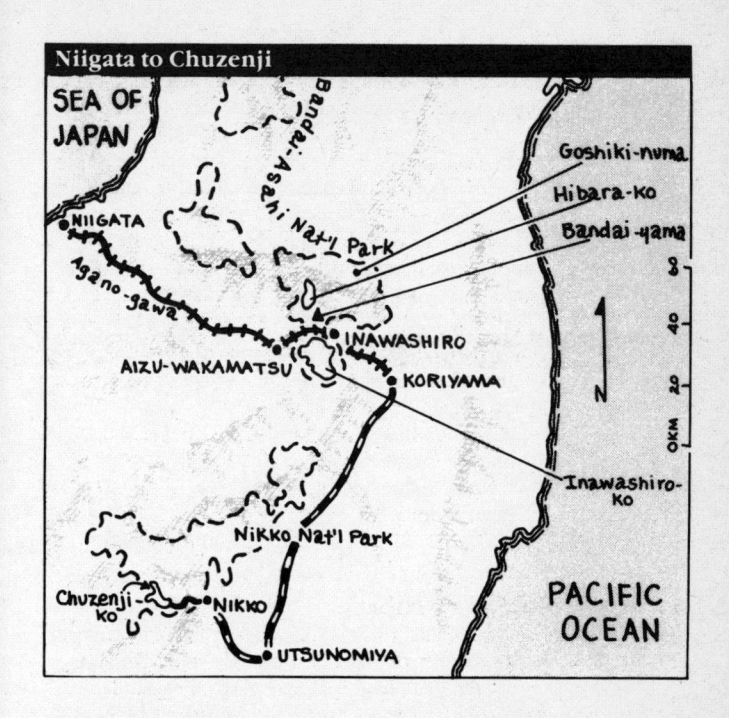

even on the map. The people are friendly and interested to see foreign faces in this neck of the woods. Be outgoing and the people will respond to you. Bandai-Kogen (the Bandai Uplands) is loaded with quiet charm and armed with magnificent views of the imposing, steamy, volcanic Bandai mountains all around.

At Inawashiro, you have a short wait for a bus that takes you up the mountain to the resort village of Ura-bandai. Call ahead from the station to tell your pension that you're on your way, 'Moshi moshi, [your last name] desu, ima Inawashiro eki ni imasu,' and they'll pick you up at the bus stop.

Sightseeing highlight

● ● **Goshiki-numa:** Five Coloured Swamp is the unglamorous name of this gorgeous series of ponds formed by the eruption of Mt Bandai in 1888. The waters run from aquamarine to blue to green and several other shades in between. There is a beautiful, spirit-lifting one-hour trek through pools, waterfalls and a profusion of trees. The trail begins (or ends) at Goshiki-numa Iriguchi and leaves you at the Bandai Kogen bus stop near the Pension.

Accommodation

The **Ura-Bandai Pension Village** has some 30 pensions. All are nice. For information contact the Ura-Bandai Pension Assoc., Ura-Bandai, Fukushima-ken, 969-27, Tel: (02413)2-2004.

Pension Hozuki, Tel: 02413-2-2724, is a lovely place nestled in the woods on a tiny lake. The beds are comfortable, and if the weather warrants it the floors are heated. Very nice for the price. The food is continental and well prepared. It would be nice to spend a week here during ski season. The hosts don't speak much English, but at this point in your trip you will manage fine anyway.

TOUR 20

TRAVEL TO NIKKO

Nearing the end of the trip, you'll discover one of the most colourful shrines in all Japan. Admire the shrines of Nikko and the natural beauty of the lake and mountains around nearby Chuzenji. Finish with a quiet evening 'at home' in your ryokan, minshuku or pension.

Suggested schedule	
7:30	Breakfast, pack and pay.
8:30	Walk the Goshiki Numa Trail.
10:15	Check out and get a ride to the bus stop.
10:45	Bus to Inawashiro Eki.
12:10	Local to Koriyama.
12:45	Arrive in Koriyama.
13:14	Leave Koriyama on Yamabiko 46 Shinkansen.
13:48	Arrive in Utsonomiya.
13:57	JR local to Nikko.
14:42	Arrive in Nikko.
	Catch the first bus up the hill to Chuzenji.

Transport

After an early breakfast, walk or ask for a ride to the bus stop, where you can catch a bus for the short trip to Goshiki Numa Iriguchi. Perhaps your hosts will give you a lift if you ask. After a one-hour hike among the lakes you'll have plenty of time to get back to the pension and collect your bags, return to the bus station, and head for Inawashiro Eki.

From there it's a straightforward train ride to Nikko.

At Nikko, catch a bus to Chuzenji in front of the station. After the many tight turns of the famous Irohasaka Road, you will top out at the village of Chuzenji. 840 yen (£3.80) for the ride.

Sightseeing highlights

● ● **Mt Nantai,** an extinct volcano, looms over the magnificent setting of lakes and mountains. For an excellent view (if the weather is clear) ride the Chanokidaira Ropeway (600 yen (£2.75)).

● ● **Lake Chuzenji:** Cold, clear, sparkling beauty, unfortunately overcrowded most of the time. Admire it without the crowds in early morning or late evening.

● ● **Chuzenji Temple:** Chu-zen-ji means 'middle zen temple'. It is located around the lake to the left, just past the French

Chuzenji

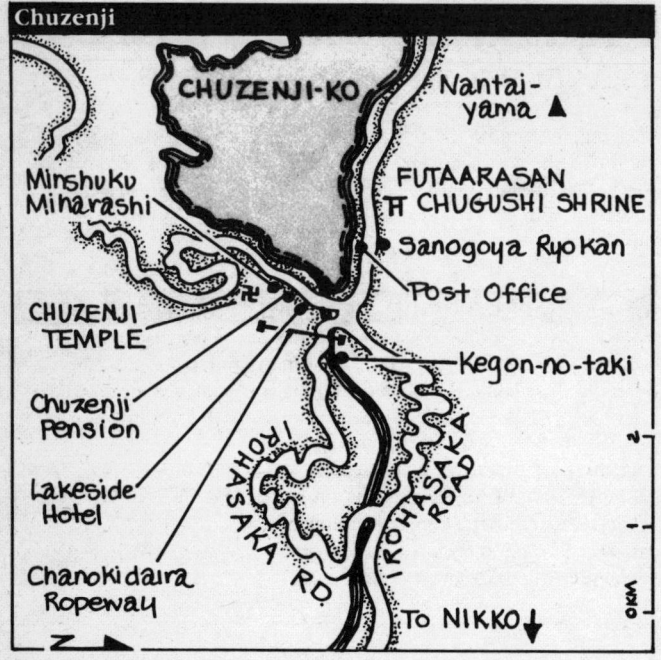

[Map showing: CHUZENJI-KO, Nantai-yama, Minshuku Miharashi, FUTAARASAN CHUGUSHI SHRINE, Sanogoya Ryokan, Post Office, CHUZENJI TEMPLE, Kegon-no-taki, Chuzenji Pension, IROHASAKA ROAD, Lakeside Hotel, IROHASAKA RD., Chanokidaira Ropeway, TO NIKKO]

Embassy's villa. You can usually get a lull between flag waving tours if you sit for a while and admire the lake. The tour of the main building and its Tachiki-kannon, which doesn't take long, provides a great view and a good place to take pictures. Climb up inside the bell tower near the entrance — don't be bashful, get up there and give that thing a wallop!

●● **Futaarasans' Chugushi Shrine:** A subdued yet elegant structure with some lovely cryptomeria trees and an enticing inner sanctum. As you stand in front of the shrine, the sanctum sanctorum is in the inner depths of a very long-looking hallway (the length is actually a rather good optical illusion to make you feel like a lowly mortal).

I had a chance to watch an elderly carpenter (daiku) re-work some of the old joinery of the shrine. He told me more and more religious structures (such as the Chuzenji temple) are being made of cement simply because there are no longer enough skilled joinery carpenters (moku-dai) who know how to make buildings like this one.

● **Kegon no Taki:** This waterfall is overrated, but since it is one of Chuzenji's best-known tourist sights (and right by the bus depot) you might as well take a look. The bottom viewing platform can only be reached by lift (500 yen (£2.25)). Crowded.

Accommodation
Sanogoya Ryokan, Tochigi ken, Nikko shi, Chugu shi, 2478
Tel: 0288-55-0091. When you arrive in Chuzenji, stay on the bus
past the bus station at Kegon Falls and ride along the lake to the
post office (yubin kyoku basu tei). If you get to Futaarasan Shrine
on the edge of town you've gone one stop too far; walk back.
Between the post office and a shop selling drink you'll find a
cement path that leads up the hill. Walk up it and the ryokan is
to the right. Tourist town prices prevail here — 7,500 yen (£34) a
night. Sanogoya has one of the few authentic wooden o-furo I've
seen in a long time. Good food and a nice view of the lake.

   Chuzenji Pension, Nikko shi, Chuzenji Kohan, 321-16, Tel:
0288-55-0720. Popular among Gaijin, it has good food and private
baths. Sudoo-san, the mistress of the house, speaks some English.
Get off at the Kegon Taki Bus Station and walk south along the
lakeshore a little less than a half a kilometre and you'll see it on
the left. 8,500 yen (£38).

   Minshuku Miharashi, Nikko shi, Chuzenji Kohan 2482, Tel:
0288-55-0103 (Makabe-san). A fine view of the lake, and
reasonable comfort. The price is right — 5,000 yen (£23). Walk
past the pension another hundred yards or so toward Chuzenji
Shrine and the minshuku is on the left.

TOUR 21

CHUZENJI/NIKKO

Enjoy a slow-paced, pleasant day. Take the bus back down the hill to the Toshogu stop and explore Nikko on foot. There are some good shops on the main road into town where you can buy a gift for the person who overwatered your plants and underfed your dog back home.

Suggested schedule	
9:00	After breakfast, catch a bus from the Kegon Station for the ride down the hill to Nikko.
Morning	See Toshogu Shrine and the Sacred Bridge.
Afternoon	Lunch in the neighbourhood, see Rinnoji and whatever else you please in Nikko.
Evening	Rest and stroll around the lake.

Sightseeing highlights—Nikko

● **Shinkyo (Sacred Bridge):** Originally reserved for the Emperor and his emissaries, this bridge is now used only on festival days. At this site the priest Shodo was said to have crossed the river on the backs of two huge snakes. The present bridge was built in 1902.

●●● **Toshogu Shrine:** Though some call it gaudy, most of us find this shrine's profusion of intricate decoration and bright colour splendid to behold. Over 15,000 craftsmen were employed in its construction, completed in 1636. Outstanding features include the Five Storey Pagoda at the entrance, and the Sanjinko (storehouse) whose unusual elephant carving was created by an artist who had never seen an elephant but relied on a literary description. The original 'Hear No Evil, See No Evil and Speak No Evil' monkey carving is nearby on the lintel of the Stables for Sacred Horses. Further in is the shrine's centrepiece, the Yomei-mon (Sunlight Gate) with its lavish carving and adornment. Purchase your ticket for the whole shrine complex at Rinnoji Temple.

● **Rinnoji Temple:** A part of the main complex, this temple of the Tendai Sect was founded in 848 by the Buddhist saint Jikaku-daishi. It contains a profusion of statues dedicated to Amida-nyorai, the Thousand Headed Kannon and Bato-Kannon. Buy your ticket for the rest of the shrine here. 1,500 yen (£7) gets you all the temples you can stand.

●● **Futaarasan Shrine:** Founded in 767 (nearly a thousand years older than Toshogu), the shrine is devoted to the divinities

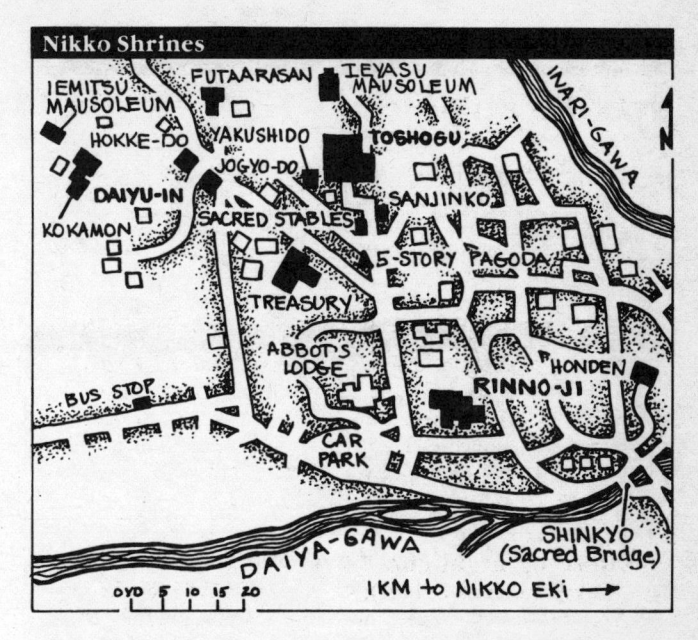

of Mt Nantai (formerly called Mt Futaara). It is in three parts:
the Honsha (main shrine), the Chugushi (middle shrine), and the
Okumiya (inner shrine) on top of Mt Nantai. For a fee you can
walk up the mountain. It is a pretty stiff walk. Inquire at the
temple's ticket window for prices. Visitors see the bright red
Honden (main hall) and the inner garden with its holy spring and
Bake-doro (goblin lantern).

Nightlife
There isn't any, unless you count the bar in the Lakeside Hotel
(it used to have slot machines — now, alas, gone the way of the
speckled-back mud dauber). Perhaps a flagon of sake would
provide consolation? The shop by the Sanno Goya is well
stocked.

Your best bet for the evening, after dinner at your
accommodation, is a romantic moonlight walk along the lakeshore;
or just sit and ponder the sights you've seen.

TOUR 22

NIKKO-TOKYO

Back to the megalopolis! A two-hour ride will return you to the place where you began nearly three weeks ago. Revisit old haunts or explore a part of the city you missed the first time through. Rest up for tomorrow's flight home.

Suggested schedule	
7:30	Have breakfast and check out.
8:20	Take the bus back down to Nikko.
10:05	JR train to Utsonomiya.
10:41	Arrive Utsonomiya and hurry for:
10:48	Shinkansen to Ueno.
11:34	Arrive in Ueno.
12:00	Lunch at Tachi Soba near Ueno station.
Afternoon	Check into your hotel, then do what you like with your last day. If you have money left, maybe go shopping in Harajuku, Shinjuku or Akihabara.

Return to Tokyo

This transport segment needs no explanation to a Nippon veteran like yourself.

As you return to your first lodgings, you'll feel that you've come full circle. Doesn't Tokyo seem different from the first time around? After a couple of weeks in the country it should seem much less strange, more like a place you could get comfortable in. If you forgot to buy gifts for the people back home, now's your last chance.

Shinjuku has several good discount camera/electronics/watch stores near the subway station. **Sakura Ya** and **Yodobashi Camera** are my favourite; haggle hard and buy several of one item to get the best deal. East down Shinjuku-dori you'll find a little of everything. The **Isetan Depaato** (department store) warrants a visit to see one of Tokyo's (and the world's) best department stores. They sell bath salts from all the major hot springs in the country — unusual, good, inexpensive gifts.

Between Yotsuya and Shinjuku is a great shop, **Bingo-ya.** Done up like an old storehouse, it's full of authentically Japanese folk art and memorabilia, such as sandals of the type sold to pilgrims at shrines. Near the Dai-Ichii Hospital off Shinjuku-dori.

Akihabara offers electronics galore. Great for household appliances, stereo equipment and toys. Wander and be amazed at how many shops there are. Go back into the little alley-like shopping arcades where you can find everything from fuses to phone taps.

In Harajuku, shop in **Kiddyland** for toys and the neighbouring **Oriental Bazaar** for all those oriental nick-nacks people back home ask for, such as swords, kimonos and T-shirts. There are many other good shops in this district as well.

Return home

Most UK bound flights leave in the afternoon or early evening from Narita Airport. Remember that two hour ride to the airport and leave yourself plenty of time. The easiest way to get out of town is to catch an Airport Express from the New Otani. Call there and ask the receptionist for details.

Returning home the jet lag is always worse for some reason. (This is a documented fact, not some personal delusion!) For the first few days you may find yourself falling asleep early, then waking up in the middle of the night with sleep nowhere in sight. It can be maddening, but don't worry — it will pass.

POST TOUR OPTION

HOKKAIDO

Hokkaido should be part of any tour to Japan. It wouldn't fit in the main itinerary, though, without rushing you at a frantic pace through the rest of the country. Better to see some of Japan at your leisure, rather than more of it at a mad dash. Given an extra week you can enjoy Hokkaido too.

Before the mid-19th century, Hokkaido was a backwater inhabited by the aboriginal Ainu tribe and by outcasts from mainstream Japanese society. The vast mineral and natural resource wealth of Hokkaido changed all that when, in 1868, the Emperor invited economic development advisers from the US administration of President Grant. The rugged land and colder weather gave Hokkaido a character similar in many ways to America's western frontier.

Hokkaido's terrain is more alpine, and the people are inclined to be a bit rough and rustic. They are generally very outgoing and friendly as well.

Hokkaido doesn't have the ancient temples or lore-shrouded shrines of the southern islands. Instead it offers a natural splendour altogether different from anywhere else in Japan. Its wide open spaces, spectacular vistas and many hot springs provide welcome relief from the bustling crowds of the southern islands.

Transport

If you intend to see Hokkaido, get a one-week extension for your rail pass at the time of purchase for about £100. Or an Excursion Pass (Shuyuken), available within Japan but not in Hokkaido itself, gives reduced rates for fixed-itinerary travel. The rate varies with your proposed route and length of stay but it does offer fairly substantial savings. It must be purchased down south at major JR (Japan Railway) offices. Tokyo would be the obvious choice.

From Tokyo you can either fly to Sapporo in an hour for about £60, or ride the trains and ferry for fifteen hours. If you opt to fly, purchase a ticket at any JTB office. Flights north (as well as almost all domestic routes) leave from the old Haneda Airport. It's a half hour from downtown Tokyo by the monorail that leaves from Hamamatsucho Station on the Yamanote line. The trip north overland is interesting enough, though it does not rival the scenery you've already seen in other parts of Japan. Ideally you would fly one way and take the train the other way.

Post Tour Option

Hokkaido

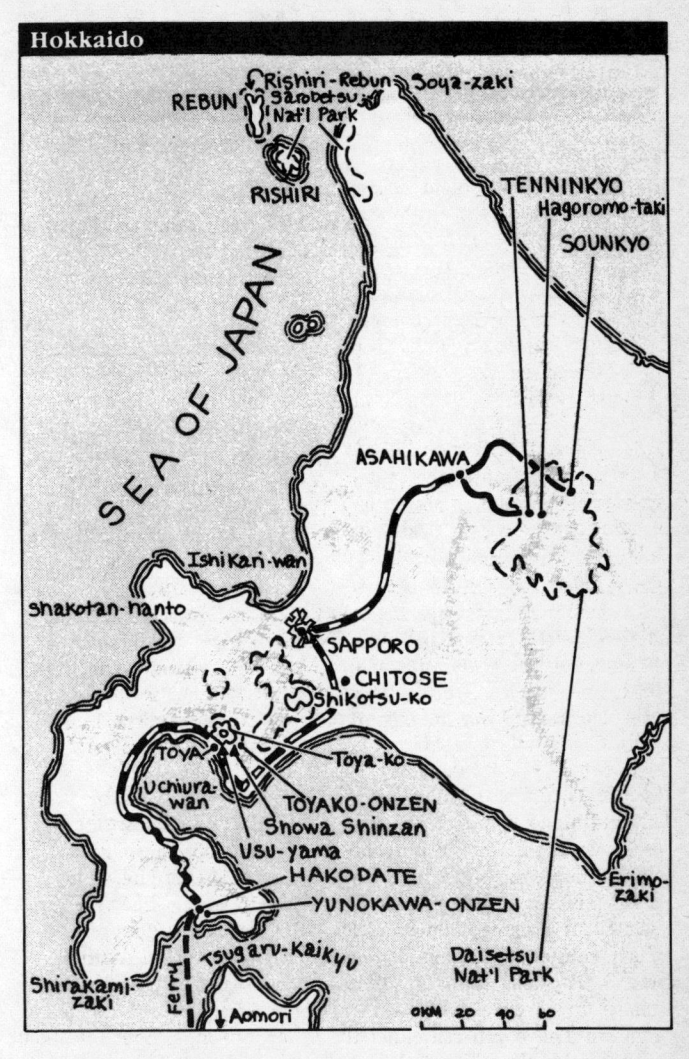

Heading north, it is convenient to see some of the highlights on the way. Stops also help to break up the long trip. A sample itinerary for the ride north follows.

DAY 1: TOKYO TO HAKODATE

Suggested schedule

8:40	Leave Ueno Eki for Morioka on the Yamabiko Shinkansen.
11:25	Arrive in Morioka.
11:36	Depart Morioka on LEX Hatsukari, arriving in Aomori at 14:02.
14:50	Seikan Ferry to Hakodate. Arrive at 18:45.
19:02	Hokuto 9 to Sapporo. Arrive at 23:02.
Evening	Dinner in and to bed.

Transport

All connections are straightforward and well-marked on this major trunk route. The ferry connection is simple: get off the train and walk down a ramp to the boat. It is possible to get a night train to Sapporo if you can stand that much train riding.

The port town of Hakodate isn't a major tourist attraction — a hot spring resort and plenty of places to stay but nothing exceptional. The evening will be quiet.

Sightseeing highlights: Hakodate

- **Asa-ichii:** The morning market, just down the street from the station, is full of produce, fish and crabs. Food stands on the pavement serve kegani (hairy crab) — the freshest, sweetest shelfish you'll ever eat. Great for a late breakfast.

A fellow here named Yoori is a self-taught linguist. He loves Spanish, English and Italian and will have a go at any others you might know and care to try him on. See if he speaks Swahili or Serbo-Croatian. Yoori's stand is right in the front centre of the market. Look for a guy with a big smile and a white headband. He'll most likely grab you as you walk by.

The market is open every day but Sunday.

- **Mt Hakodate Peninsula:** A short walk or taxi ride (three kilometres or so) away, this peninsula has an interesting frontier waterfront flavour, your first taste of the difference between the north and the south.

Accommodation

Kita No Yado: In nearby Yunokawa Onsen, simple but decent minshuku accommodation. Nice hotspring baths, and washing machines which may come in handy. Tel: 0138-59-2092.

Akai Boshi: A small place where Chinese and German are spoken, a ten-minute walk from the station at 3–22, Asahi cho, Hakodate 040, Tel: 0138-26-4035.

DAY 2: HAKODATE/LAKE TOYA

Suggested schedule	
8:00	Breakfast (or skip it and eat crabs at the morning market), walk along the beach.
9:00	Morning market, then see the peninsula.
11:38	LEX Otori for Toya.
13:36	Arrive in Toya, bus to Toyako Onzen.
Afternoon	Tour the splendid environs of Toya.

Transport
The 2-hour train trip to Toya takes you through pond-speckled woods and along isolated wind-swept coastline. From Hakodate, get on the train that says 'For Chitose', usually Platform 4.

In Toya, get off the train at the main terminal. A bus will probably be waiting in front of the station to take you north along the lake to Toyako Onzen resort and your lodgings. The ticket is only 120 yen (55p). It would probably be a good idea to get tomorrow's transport sorted out today.

Sightseeing highlights
● ● **Mt Showa Shinzan:** This volcano sprouted in 1944–45 in a farmer's field, much to his surprise (he'd been expecting potatoes). It continued to grow for several months, peaking at 1,300 feet. Today it still steams enough to make you wonder whether it's really dormant. At the foot of the mountain is a museum commemorating the explosion with vivid displays. Nearby Mt Usu (also reached by bus) has a multi-media show depicting the explosion. Another bus takes you to a ropeway you can ride to the summit for a good panorama of this lovely, mountainous country. The cost is 1,000 yen (£4.50). Just watching the fuming vaporoles from a distance is enough excitement for most people.

● ● ● **Lake Toya:** A round, deep, clear, gem of a lake with a cluster of islets at its centre. For 600 yen (£2.75) you can take a ferry boat and stroll around the largest, Nakanoshima, as well as the smaller islets of Kannon, Manju and Benten. The temples there aren't fantastic, but the scenery is — especially in the autumn. Buy biscuits to feed the deer and save some for swarming fish from the pier. The ferry will leave you at each island for as long as you like, then you can catch the next one that comes by.

Accommodation
Both places suggested below have volcanic hot-spring fed tubs on the premises.

Ikoiso is a typical Hokkaido minshuku — good food, clean, but not much to look at. Ano-san, the proprietor, is a great cook. Put in your request ahead of time for a Toban dinner, an individual fondue-type dish of meat, vegetables and fish left to cook in their own juices until the flame beneath burns out or you just can't bear to leave it alone anymore. Superb. The lodge has a great location on the lake, away from the large tourist hotels, about two kilometres northwest of town. 5,500 yen (£25) a night per person. The address is: Sobetsu-cho, Sobetsu Onzen, 83, Hokkaido, Tel: 01427552522.

Pension Ono has western-style beds and Japanese food for 6,000 yen (£27) a night. Satoru-san, mistress of the house, is extremely pleasant and outgoing. 56-2 Sobetsu Onzen, Sobetsu-cho, Usugun, Hokkaido, Tel: 01427-5-412.

DAY 3: TOYA-SAPPORO

Suggested schedule	
	Rise when you please and break your fast, then bus into town in time to catch the 10:30 bus to Toya Eki.
11:38	Train to Sapporo (reserve ahead).
2:00	Check into your hotel.
2:30	See some of Sapporo.
6:30	Bathe and get ready for a night out on the town: Susukino and thereabouts.

Transport
If Toyako-onzen seems crowded, reserve your return bus ticket to Toya the afternoon you arrive or first thing the next morning. You have a short wait in Toya for your train to the big city, a 1½-hour ride through fairly interesting countryside.

Sapporo
This is a different kind of Japanese town. Laid out by American engineers and Japanese in western style, it is — believe it or not — square. You can find your way easily to anywhere on the map!

Pick up a copy of 'Welcome to Sapporo' from the JTB office just down the street (Sapporo Dori) from the station. This is the easiest to use and most comprehensive map of Sapporo; it's also free. Sapporo Dori, the main north/south axis of the city, is intersected mid-town by Odori-park. The area bounded by the university to the north and Nakajima Park to the south is the centre of attraction for out-of-towners, fun and delightfully easy to get around.

Sightseeing highlights
● **The Old Clock Tower:** One block east of Sapporo Dori and three blocks south of the Sapporo Station, this is Sapporo's only surviving example of Russian architecture. It was built in 1881 and now houses a library and an exhibit on the early days of Hokkaido.

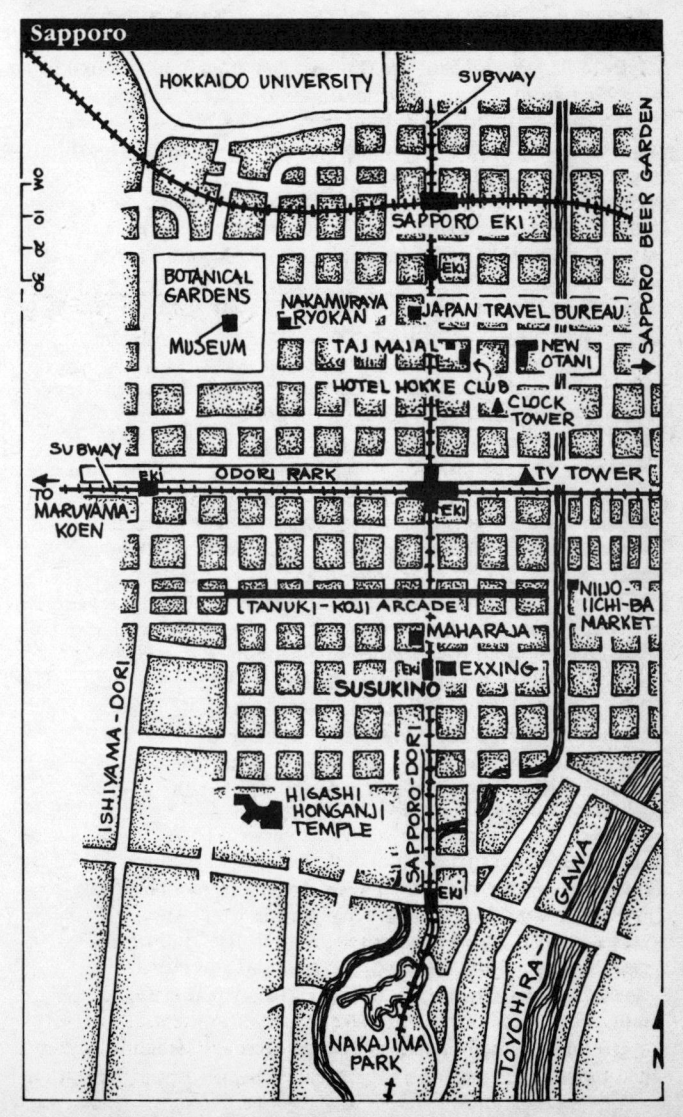

● ● **Botanical Gardens:** Just west of the station, this park is jammed with all the flora and some of the fauna of Hokkaido. A great place for a picnic, with lovely walking trails through woods, meadows and swamplands. Also in the park are the Ainu Museum (presently closed) and, next door, the University Museum where for 100 yen (45p) you can see the rather bedraggled but unusual bird collection of British ornithologist T.W. Blakiston. Admission to the park is 300 yen (£1.35).

● **Pole Town and Aurora Town:** Two huge underground shopping arcades. Fun to wander around in, they epitomise underground life in Japan. Find them by descending into the subway in the residential area. Shops and restaurants, including the ubiquitous McD's.

● ● **Maruyama-Koen:** 140 yen (65p) will get you a subway ticket from the residential neighbourhood to this park south of town. The southbound subway platform is down on the second sub level, just north of Pole Town. The signs are mostly in English, so finding it is no great task. Get off at Maruyama Koen station and walk west to the park. Once there, head for the elegant Hokkaido Shrine in the centre of the park. It has the power and grace of the big shrines down south, but with heavy-weather durability.

● **Moiwa Ropeway:** You can get a taxi from the Hokkaido Shrine to the ropeway. If the weather is good, the view from the top is grand. The full ticket, 1,200 yen (£5.45) per adult, also lets you ride a little chairlift to enjoy 'free' telescopes atop the viewing platform. If that seems a bit expensive, just buy the ropeway ticket for 800 yen (£3.65) and walk at the top.

● **Tannuki Koji Arcade:.** This arcade, enclosed and above ground, has antique and miscellaneous shops at the west end. Gojyo Sakana Tsuuri-ya, the fishing shop on the second block from the west end, is famous in Japan. Mr Gojyo is the man who makes £2,000 fishing rods of bamboo and silk. He doesn't speak English, but if you say, 'Aiyu tsuri no bideo o chotto misete kudasai' he may show you a video of this unusual kind of fishing and how his rods are made. Across the street is the most remarkably packed antique store you've ever seen.

Accommodation

Nakamuraya Ryokan: Conveniently located one block east of the botanical gardens, this is a standard inn for Gaijin. Good food and friendly people. Priced from 5,500 yen (£25) up. Nishi 7, Chuo ku, Sapporo City 060-01, Tel: 011-241-2111.

Hotel Hokke Club: Tel: 011-221-2141. 7,000 yen (£32) per night.

New Otani Sapporo: Fine rooms, excellent service — a very good hotel, well located in north central Sapporo near the station.

If you are a New Otani Member from your stay in Tokyo, stay here. Tel: 011-222-1111.

Food
Taj Majal Indian Restaurant: Between the Chisan Hotel and the Hotel Tokeidai. Mr Raza, the manager, got me started in Sapporo with a great lunch, then found me a hotel when there were none to be found. Enjoy his excellent food.

Niijo-iichi-ba market: A bustling fish and produce market full of goodies from crab and smoked salmon to Sunkist lemons. (The three go exceptionally well together for a picnic in the park or in your hotel room. Hmmm... save some money and eat well.)

Sapporo Beer Garden: The order of the day here is Ghengis Khan (Gengisu Kan), named of course, after a famous Mongolian who apparently loved nothing better than to eat sheep and drink large quantities of beer. The old Sapporo Beer Brewery is the scene of Octoberfest-like drinking and eating. The waiter brings out large platters of meat, fish and vegetables which you then cook on a table barbecue. In the summer you can do all this outdoors for even more fun.

Nightlife
After dinner, walk into Susukino for nightlife. Susukino, by the way, is a type of marsh reed that flourished in the area before the locals decided they needed more nightclubs. More neon than anyplace this side of the Ginza, worth seeing at night even if you're not the slightest bit interested in drinking and carousing. If, on the other hand, you *are* interested, you've definitely come to the right place.

Noteworthy clubs in this area are **Club Exxing** and **The Maharaja.** I prefer Exxing, which advertises (for some reason) 'Neurotic Romance'. Big dance floor, great lighting. Admission (4,000 yen (£18)) includes enough coupons to get yourself thoroughly filled with the liquid of your choice, plus food from a decent sushi bar. The Maharaja enjoys a more lively clientele on some days, but the management is not nearly as outgoing and flamboyant as at Exxing. It is, however, one of *the* nightclubs in Sapporo. Another 'in' club is the **Signife' Club.** Look for the sign under the neon Asahi Beer sign in the middle of Susukino. Each place costs around 4,000 yen (£18).

DAY 4: TENNINKYO

Suggested schedule	
7:00	Check out and head for Sapporo Eki.
8:00	Train for Asahikawa.
9:30	Arrive and wait for the free bus to the Spa.
10:05	Bus to Tenninkyo.
11:00	Arrive at Tenninkyo and walk up the hill to your hotel.
	Note: Rail and bus timetables change with seasons in Hokkaido so always check the specified times at a JTB office or at the Midori no Madoguchi ticket window.

Tenninkyo: Tenninkyo, a morning's travel north from Sapporo in the Daisetsuzan National Park, is a quiet, unassuming spa with indoor and outdoor (rotenburo) hot springs, old ramshackle hotels and a stunning waterfall nearby. It is one of *the* places to see the autumn colours in Japan. The only thing wild about this place is the beauty of the gorge that surrounds it. The angular rock spires which line the road give a very distinctive feel to this entire area. This area is remote and for probably the first time on this trip you'll be at the end of the road.

Transport
Tenninkyo is easy to reach. At Asahikawa, walk out of the train station and you'll see a bus stand slightly off to the right on the street. The far right hand stop is for Tenninkyo. The ride is free to hotel guests. The early bus will be full of locals, pretty colourful country folk, returning home from morning shopping. One hour on the bus through magnificent scenery and you're there.

The Daisetsuzan area, although well touristed, doesn't have the public transport you've grown accustomed to in the southern islands. A hire car would be a great way to see this entire area. Without one, buses will have to suffice for reaching the more remote parts of the interior. Explore; just don't do it so late in the day that you can't get a bus back to your accommodation. I've even had good luck hitchhiking, but it's a purely hit-or-miss proposition.

Sightseeing highlights
●●● Walk up the valley (with picnic lunch in hand, perhaps), to see the truly gorgeous **Hagoromono Taki**. This waterfall is breathtaking, particularly in autumn. Further up the valley is another waterfall, unfortunately marred by an inaccessible steel

bridge that goes up the valley. Walk, enjoy the scenery, and then go back and soak your bones in an outdoor tub (rotenburo).

Accommodation
All the hotels in this valley have similar accommodation. The prices are rather high everywhere, due to the limited availability of rooms.

Tenninkyo Grand Hotel (Kamikawa gun, biei cho, Tenninkyo Onzen, Kamikawa. Tel: 01669-6-2311) has the most extensive bathing facilities. About 10,000 yen (£45) per person, two meals and baths included.

Tenninkaku: Tenninkyo-onsen, Higashikawa cho, Kawakumi gun 071-03, Tel: 0166-97-2111. 10,000 to 15,000 yen (£45 to £70).

Return to Sapporo or go on to Sounkyo

DAY 5: SAPPORO TO SOUNKYO
The transport on this segment is easy. Stations are small, everything is clearly marked and finding buses is easy. From Tenninkyo to Sounkyo, take the first convenient bus (they run hourly) to Asahikawa. From there get on the first convenient bus up the valley to Sounkyo. There is frequent service on this route and you should have no trouble finding the buses in front of the station.

Fantastic ice-carved rock spires and thin cataracts of water line the Sounkyo Gorge. Everywhere you look there's something magnificent. Autumn colours are awesome.

Suggested schedule	
7:00	Check out and off to the station.
8:00	Leave for Asahikawa.
9:41	Arrive in Asahikawa.
9:50	Bus to Sounkyo.
11:40	Arrive in Sounkyo, check into accommodation.
12:00	Ropeway to the top of Mt Daisetsu, walk for a few hours.
Afternoon	Walk in the park, take a bus into the inner park. Explore. Chujo Setsuri is a spot worth finding as is Lake Mashuko.
Evening	Eat, bathe and relax.

Sightseeing highlights
On the bus ride, you'll pass **Ryusei no taki** and **Ginga no taki**, two lovely waterfalls.

Take another bus up the canyon from Sounkyo Onzen to **Kobako** and **Obako** ('Little Box' and 'Big Box'; as you might guess, these are box canyons). See the sights early or late in the day without the crowds.

● ● **Mt Daisetsu Ropeway:** 1,300 (£6) gets you a ride to the top of the hill, with a commanding view and great hiking on the ridges behind the ropeway station. Take a picnic lunch and walk. The trails are well marked.

● ● **Mashuko:** A small lake in the park, a short bus ride from town, is also a nice place for a picnic.

Last words

Other places well worth seeing in Hokkaido, given enough time and money, are **Akan National Park**, the **Shakotan Peninsula** near Sapporo, the **Shiretoko Peninsula** on the east coast, and the remote islands of **Rishiri** and **Rebun** on the north coast. Sorry, I can't cover it all in this little book (nor will you be able to in a single trip).

Returning south to Tokyo by train is simple. Go to the JTB office at Sapporo Eki to book your trip the day before you want to leave. If you plan to fly, get a ticket from the JTB and head for Chitose Airport. After a month of travelling in Japan this will pose no problem for you. By now you know how easy getting around in Japan really is.

BRIEF HISTORY OF JAPAN

Japan, once part of the Asian mainland, fell off into the Pacific (as some people predict California will) in a series of earthquakes about 20,000 years ago. Anthropologists believe early people migrated to the islands across land bridges from Korea and Siberia during the last Ice Age, as well as by boat from Polynesia.

100–600 AD: Jimmu Tenno, the semi-mythical emperor who was the Japanese counterpart to Britain's King Arthur, formed a kingdom called Yamato, with its capital somewhere between Kyoto and Nara — it was customary to move the capital each time an emperor died. The Japanese racial identity dates from the Yamato Period, as do the Shinto religion, the subservience of women, and ritual bathing.

The **Geku** or Outer Shrine at Ise dates back to the Yamato Period — 478 AD; the **Naiku** or Inner Shrine is even older, built in the year 5 BC.

600–794: The imperial bureaucracy had become too large to relocate upon the emperor's death, and the first permanent capital was established in **Nara**. The **Horyu-ji** (oldest intact Buddhist temple in Japan), **Kasuga Shrine** and **Kokuho-kan** (Treasure Hall) were built during the Nara Period. Buddhism was declared to be the national religion, and in 756 AD the **Todaiji Temple** and its **Daibutsu** (Great Buddha) were completed. Just 28 years later the new emperor, Kammu, decided to move the capital from Nara to Kyoto. Also built during this period were the original **Asakusa-Kannon Temple**, the reconstruction of which can be seen in Tokyo, and the **Futaarasan Shrine** at Nikko.

794–1182: The 400-year Heian Period, while the capital was in **Kyoto**, saw the empire expand rapidly to control most of modern-day Japan. The emperors devoted most of their time to studying Buddhism, art and literature, while the land was actually ruled by competing aristocratic families (notably the Fujiwara family) through shoguns (generals) and samurai (warriors). Also in this period, a peculiarly Japanese theology evolved which held that the ancient Shinto gods were manifestations of the Buddha, therefore people could be Shinto and Buddhist at the same time.

Kofukuji Temple and **Kasuga Shrine** in Nara were originally built by the Fujiwara family in 710 and belonged to them throughout the Heian Period; the temple has been destroyed and faithfully reconstructed twice. **Itsukushima Shrine** at Miyajima also dates back to this period.

1182–1543: Japan's capital moved to Kamakura, just south of modern-day Tokyo, where the great shogun Yoritomo Minamoto, and later his sons, ruled. In 1281, Kublai Khan invaded Japan with a force of more than 100,000 Mongol soldiers. Accompanying Kublai Khan was Marco Polo, who later described Japan for the first time to European readers. During a great battle at **Hakata** a typhoon struck, sweeping both Mongol and Japanese armies into the sea and ending the invasion. The typhoon was called 'Kamikaze' ('Divine wind').

The rulers at Kamakura failed to pay the surviving samurai and lost their allegiance, and Japan plunged into a series of civil wars. In 1335 Emperor Godaigo took control of part of the army, but three years later shogun Takauji Ashikaga drove the emperor into the mountains and formed his own court at Kyoto. Many of Kyoto's great pavilions and temples were built during this Muromachi Period (1335–1572) by Takauji and his successors. After Takauji's death warlords struggled in continuous civil war for over 100 years.

1543–49: The first Portuguese ships arrived in Japan, bringing Catholic missionaries who attempted to manipulate the warlords against each other and competed with the Buddhists for power. The Europeans also brought firearms, a few of which they sold to the warlords at astonishingly high prices. Within a few years the Japanese had copied the new technology and were producing good quality guns of their own. (Sounds familiar?)

1573–1600: Civil strife continued as powerful warlords, particularly Nobunaga Oda and his successor Toyotomi Hideyoshi (who built Miyajima's **Hall of a Thousand Mats**), struggled unsuccessfully to restore the shogunate. During this era, the Azuchi-Momoyama Period, Japan's greatest castles were built or expanded (the **Castle of the White Heron** in Himeji was first built in the 14th century, but reached its present massive size during the Azuchi-Momoyama Period) and firearms were first used in warfare. It was also a time of bold artistic development, including popularisation of **Kabuki** theatre and the chanoyu (tea ceremony).

1603–1867: The Edo Period began when Ieyasu Tokugawa conquered all rivals to become the most powerful shogun in Japanese history. He moved the government to the fortified town of Edo, later renamed Tokyo. Missionaries and traders from Europe were arriving in increasing numbers (These included William Adams, the prototype for 'Anjim-san', hero of the best-selling though historically inaccurate novel *Shogun,* who lived in

the town of Ito on the Izu Peninsula). Meanwhile, several
Japanese warlords converted to Christianity and sent emissaries to
the Pope in Rome by way of Mexico. A Jesuit-inspired
insurrection, combined with concern that a Papal bull dividing
colonisation rights to the entire world between Spain and Portugal
might mean attempts to colonise Japan, led the shogun to banish
all Europeans. Only the Dutch, who were not Roman Catholics,
were allowed a small trading colony on Dejima Island in Nagisaki
Harbour; this island was Japan's only contact with western
civilisation for over two centuries.

Ieyasu Tokugawa built the **Nijo Castle** (1603) and **Kiyomizu
Terra** (1633), both in Kyoto. Nikko's **Rinnoji Temple** and
Sacred Bridge (built on the site where earlier sacred bridges had
existed since antiquity) date from the same period, as does the
Kompira Shrine at Kotohira. The incident of the '47 Ronin',
commemorated by **Sengakuji Temple** in Tokyo, occurred in
1703.

The Edo Period was one of 'law and order' in the extreme.
Large numbers of samurai were stationed throughout the country
to prevent opponents from organising against the shogunate. They
also oppressed the peasants, victimising them with impunity and
sometimes executing people for 'crimes' of disrespect or bad
manners. There were no wars, internal or external, and many
samurai became wandering soldiers of fortune, while others
became more skilled in the tea ceremony than in the martial arts.
Meanwhile, the nation's wealth became concentrated in the rising
merchant class. By the early 19th century the shogun lacked
power to do anything besides exploit his peasantry.

Then ships from the west started arriving again.

Russian traders to Hokkaido came first, followed by a fleet of
American 'black ships' under the command of Admiral Perry,
who opened trade with Japan by threat of force. When a trade
agreement was signed with the US in 1853 and Townsend Harris
became the first American ambassador to Japan, several European
nations sought to establish trade relations in the same way: by
force. British ships bombarded Kagoshima in 1863, and the
following year a joint British, Dutch and French fleet invaded.
His weakness obvious to the people of Japan, the shogun's power
collapsed.

At Shimoda on the Izu Peninsula you'll see **Hofukuji Temple**,
dedicated to US Ambassador Harris' Japanese mistress.

1867–1912: The Imperial family, which had survived in
powerless seclusion behind palace walls in Kyoto for 250 years,
suddenly became the only semblance of government in Japan —
and the only leadership with whom the outside world could
establish diplomatic relations. In 1867 Emperor Meiji, often

called 'the monarch of modern Japan', ascended the throne. Meiji promptly moved the Imperial Court to the shogunate capital of Edo, renamed the capital city Tokyo (which means 'eastern capital'), declared Shinto the state religion (one of its tenets being that the Emperor was divine and his decrees infallible), abolished the feudal samurai system and declared the warlords' holdings forfeit to the Emperor — quite a coup, considering that few people had even realised Japan still *had* an emperor.

Meiji ruled for 45 years, during which time Japan enthusiastically embraced western science — telephones, electric lights and that most powerful symbol of modern technology, railways. Many Japanese scholars (including the artists exhibited at the **Bridgestone Museum**) travelled to Europe to study, and it became fashionable for Japanese men to marry Gaijin women. Japan also began to emerge as a military power and waged war outside her own borders for the first time. Winning wars against China (1894-95) and Russia (1904-05), Japan gained control over the island of Formosa and portions of the Asian mainland.

Tokyo's **Meiji Shrine** was built soon after the Emperor's death in 1912.

1912 – 1925: Upon Meiji's death, his son Taisho took the imperial throne. Taisho became ill and was rarely seen, but capable ministers ruled in his name. Japan entered World War I on the side of the Allies and continued to develop military strength. After the war, relations with the USA deteriorated, largely because the US passed laws denying American citizenship to the growing number of Japanese immigrants and restricting them from buying or owning land. In 1923 the Kanto earthquake struck Japan, destroying much of Tokyo and Yokohama and killing over 100,000 people. It was the worst natural disaster of modern times.

1926 – 45: Hirohito, who had studied and travelled extensively in Europe before becoming Emperor, adopted the militaristic attitudes of pre-WWII Europe. Japan's growing military power was patterned after that of Germany. Beginning in 1931, Japan expanded her empire by invading Manchuria and China. In 1940 Japan officially made an alliance with Hitler's Germany. By bombing Pearl Harbour late in 1941, Japan became locked in a four-year-long death struggle with the USA which raged across most of the Pacific Ocean until, in 1945, the US dropped atomic bombs on Hiroshima and Nagasaki, and Japan surrendered. **Peace Park** in Hiroshima memorialises the victims of the world's first sample of nuclear war.

1946-present: After World War II ended, the Japanese faced starvation, economic ruin and military occupation by the USA and the USSR. The US poured reconstruction funds into Japan in unprecedented amounts, and this financing together with the fanatical work ethic of the Japanese people created an industrial base which has come to rival even that of the US. Today Japan, with no military capability, has emerged as the second-greatest industrial power in the world, stronger economically than any European, Arabic or Communist nation. Japan's government today is a constitutional monarchy. The seat of government is in the National Diet, in central Tokyo across from the Imperial Palace. The Emperor, a figurehead much like the Queen with limited real power, belongs to the unbroken line of Emperors that can be traced back to the same time as the Roman Empire in Europe.

The **Imperial Palace** in Tokyo, which was destroyed by firebombing during World War II, was rebuilt during the 1960s using modern materials and traditional architecture.

LANGUAGE

You can get by as a tourist in Japan speaking virtually no Japanese at all — but you will enjoy yourself much more if you learn a little of the language.

Pronunciation

Japanese is a difficult language, no two ways about it. But at least, unlike some others such as Chinese, it is easily pronounceable. Once you learn the basic sounds of the language, you should be able to read words from a dictionary or phrasebook and say them so that they will be intelligible to the average man on the street.

The vowels, predominant in Japanese, are the key to pronunciation. Nearly all words end with a vowel or an 'n' sound.

A: pronounced as in 'Ahh' at the doctor's surgery.
E: the e is pronounced as in left.
I: pronounced as 'ee' as in 'eek, a mouse!'
O: a regular o as in 'Oh, I love your new pearls!'
U: sounds like the 'u' in lunatic.

The 'n' sound is a long drawn out nnnn... as if you were saying thoughtfully, 'Nnno... I don't think so'.

Other sounds that give Gaijin trouble are 'tsu' and the 'r' sounds 'ra', 'ri', 'ru', 're' and 'ro', 'Tsu' is a 'su' sound with a soft touch of 't' at the beginning. Pronounce it starting with your tongue at the roof of your mouth and touching the tops of your front teeth. The 'r' sound in Japanese is slightly rolled as in Spanish. If you can't manage that feat of linguistic prestidigitation, don't worry about it overly much; it won't keep you from being understood.

The biggest trick to correct Japanese pronunciation is: Stress all syllables equally. Say 'sa-ya-no-ra', not 'SAY-a-NOR-a'.

Using a phrasebook

Mentally practise saying words you read in a phrasebook to yourself a couple of times before you blurt them out. Short words should give you little trouble; longer ones may take a little more time to master. Learn a few. Some phrases will be used over and over again on a daily basis and you'll remember them quickly.

The biggest problem with a phrasebook is that while it may help you ask questions, the answers come at nearly the speed of light and likely as not, are completely unintelligible. Try to have an idea of what kind of answer to expect and be waiting for it. For example, when asking directions, the answer is quite likely to

Japanese grammar

It's nothing like English, and way beyond the scope of even a full phrasebook. Personal pronouns such as 'I' and 'you' are at the beginning of a sentence (usually); object nouns, participles and all the rest go in the middle, while the verbs tend to bunch up at the end of the sentence. Learn a few phrases by rote and let the general structure sink in as you go along.

Reading Japanese

Japanese 'letters' represent syllables. The written syllabaries of *hiragana* (used for all Japanese words) and *katakana* (used for foreign words) sound like this: 'a, i, u, e, o, ka, ki, ku, ke, ko, sa, shi, su, se, so, ta, chi, tsu, te, to. .' etc. You could learn both in a week if you set your mind to it, and that would let you to read things like menus and train station signs, not exactly relieving your illiteracy but at least taking the edge off it. Hiragana and katakana are both contained in appendices to most small dictionaries. If you become familiar with all the sounds in the syllabaries, you will have Japanese pronunciation down pat.

Here are some words and phrases you'll find useful in your travels:

yes Hai *(hi)*   **No** Iie. *(ee ye)*

Numbers

 1 iichi
 2 ni
 3 san
 4 shi (becomes 'yon' after ten)
 5 go
 6 roku
 7 shichi or nana
 8 hachi
 9 ku
10 ju
11 juiichi
12 juni
13 jusan
14 juyon
15 jugo
16 juroku
17 jushichi
18 juhachi
19 juku

contain words such as north, south, east and west, up and down, right, left, lift or stairs.

20	niju
21	niju iichi
22	niju ni
23	niju san
24	niju yon
	(and so on, adding numbers to the word for twenty)
30	sanju
	(37 would be three tens seven, sanju nana — confusing at first but really very simple)
40	yonju
50	goju
60	rokuju
70	nanaju
80	hachiju
90	kuju
100	hyaku
110	hyaku ju
115	hyaku ju go
120	hyaku niju
130	hyaku sanju
200	nihyaku
300	sanbyaku
400	yonhyaku
500	gohyaku
600	rophyaku
700	nanahyaku
800	hapyaku
900	kuhyaku
1,000	sen
1,150	sen hyaku goju
2,000	nisen
3,000	sansen
4,000	yonsen
5,000	gosen
6,000	rokusen
7,000	nanasen
8,000	hasen
9,000	kusen
10,000	iichiman
50,000	goman
80,000	hachiman
100,000	juman
1,000,000	hyakuman
10,000,000	senman
100,000,000	iichioku

DATES

January	iichigatsu
February	nigatsu
March	sangatsu
April	shigatsu
May	gogatsu
June	rokugatsu
July	shichigatsu
August	hachigatsu
September	kugatsu
October	jugatsu
November	juiichigatsu
December	junigatsu

(Note that the months are numbered instead of named. June 21 is 'rokugatsu niju iichi niichi' ('Sixth month, twenty first day'). In this context 'niichi' means "day.")

DAYS OF THE WEEK

Sunday	Nichiyobi	**Thursday**	Mokuyobi
Monday	Getsuyobi	**Friday**	Kinyobi
Tuesday	Kayobi	**Saturday**	Doyobi
Wednesday	Suiyobi		

SEASONS

spring	haru	**autumn**	aki
summer	natsu	**winter**	fuyu

TIMES

morning	asa	**tomorrow**	ashita
afternoon	hiru	**yesterday**	kino
evening	yube	**day after tomorrow**	asatte
night	yoru		
this morning	kesa	**day before yesterday**	ototoi
today	kiyo		
tonight	konban	**this year**	kotoshi
now	ima	**next year**	rainen
later	ato de	**last year**	kyonen
before	mae ni		

The most important words in any language are those that ask how to say the next word you might need. Rather than look every word up in the dictionary, it's easier to point at something and say, 'what is that in Japanese?'

Nihongo de kore wa nan desuka? What is this in Japanese? (literally, 'Japanese in, this is what?')
Nihongo de 'rice' wa nan to yu imi desuka? How do you say 'rice' in Japanese?
Nihongo de, rice wa gohan desu. In Japanese, rice is 'gohan'.

Two words appear at the end of many Japanese sentences: 'desu' and 'desuka' (pronounced 'des' and 'deska'. The u sound is nearly silent.) 'Desuka' makes a sentence into a question:
Kore wa nan desuka? What is this?
Kore wa Gohan desu. This is rice.
Without the 'ka', 'desu' is the equivalent of the word 'is' in English. It also serves as emphasis, ending a sentence firmly:
Kore wa hon desu. This is a book.

Other verbs also become questions when '-ka' is added to the end:
How much? Ikura desuka?
You can get the price of nearly anything you can point to simply by saying, 'ikura desuka?'
Equally important when shopping for tourist type items such as cameras and watches, is the phrase:
Can you give me a discount? Waribiki dekimasuka?

Can you...? ...dekimasuka?
Can you speak English? Eigo ga dekimasuka?
Can you speak Japanese? Nihongo ga dekimasuka?
Yes I can. Hai dekimaso.
No, I can't speak Japanese. Iie, Nihongo ga dekimasen.
('Iie', pronounced 'ee-ye', means no. 'Nihon' means 'Japan' and 'go' means language, so 'Nihongo' is 'Japanese', 'Eikoku' is 'England', so 'Eigo' means 'English'.)

Do you have...? ...arimasuka?
Do you have sushi? Sushi ga arimasuka?
Do you have a room? Heya ga arimasuka?
Yes, we do. Hai, heya ga arimasu.
We have no room. Iie, heya ga arimasen.
(By adding the '-sen' suffix, the verb becomes negative. Another way of saying 'We have no room' is 'Chotto main desu'. This really means, 'We are a little full'. A polite way of saying the same unpleasant thing.)

Where is...? Doko desuka?
Where is the toilet? Toirei wa doko desuka?
Where is the station? Eki wa doko desuka?
Where is the policeman? Keisatsu wa doko desuka?
Where is a hotel? Oteru wa doko desuka?
Where is a minshuku? Minshuku wa doko desuka?
Where is a bank? Ginko wa doko desuka?
Where is the bus stop? Basu tei wa doko desuka?

'Kudasai' means 'please' or 'to receive'. You can ask for all kinds of things with this handy word:
Tempura noodles, please. Tempura soba kudasai.
Ramen noodles, please. Ramen kudasai.
Coffee, please. Kohii kudasai.

Good Ii
Is it good?(or)Is it all right? Ii desuka?
Often a solicitous housemother will ask, 'Iiii?' 'Good? Is everything alright?'
Yes it is fine (good). Hai, ii desu.

Delicious Oishi
Your host will look at you and say 'Oishi?' This means 'Do you like it? Is it good?'
If you like it say 'Oishi'.
If you *really* like it, try 'Sugoku oishi'. (Very delicious'.)
If it is not delicious, say 'Oishikunai'. (The 'nai' at the end of 'oishi' does the same as 'sen' on 'dekimasen' — it makes a negative. 'Not delicious'. *Very* seldom would a Japanese person come right out and say 'Oishikunai'.)

SOME FOOD WORDS
chopsticks	o-hashi
sweet (or) delicious	amai
sour	Supai
spicy hot	karai
bitter	nigai
flavour	aji
hot	atsui
cold (food or drink)	sumetai
	('Cold' (weather) is 'samui')
I'm hungry	Onaka suita (My stomach is empty)
I'm thirsty	Nodo ga itai (My throat hurts)
I'm full	Onaka ipai

ACCOMMODATION
hotel	oteru
minshuku	minshuku
ryokan	ryokan
Japanese room	washitsu
western-style room	yoshitsu
room w/two meals	nishoku
room charge	ryokin
reservation	yoyaku
room	heya
bathroom (toilet)	toirei
bath	o-furo
Japanese food	Nihon shoku
western food	yushoku
towel	tauru ('ta-u-ru')
slippers	suripa

TERRAIN
Mountain	yama
river	kawa
peninsula	hanto
cape	zaki
town	machi
city	shi
road	doro
bay	wan
island	shima

TRANSPORT
plane	hikoki
bus	basu
boat	fune
car	kuruma (or) jidosha
train	densha
subway	chikatetsu
walk	aruite
taxi	takushi

GREETINGS
Good morning	Ohio gozaimasu
Good day	Konichi wa
Good evening	Kon ban wa
Good night	Oyasuminasai
How do you do	Hajimemashite
Pleased to meet you	Yoroshiku
Goodbye	Sayonara
Thanks	Domo

Thank you	Arigato
Thank you very much	Domo arigato gozaimashita
Please	Kudasai
Please help, do a favour	Onegai shimasu (literally, 'I beg you')
See you later	Sore ja, mata ne
Excuse me	Gomen nasai (or) Sumimasen
I've been rude, imposed	Shitsurei shimasu (or) O jama shimashita

HEALTH

hurt(s)	itai
sick	byoki
headache	atama ga itai
stomach ache	onaka ga itai
sore throat	nodo ga itai
Please help me	tetsudaite kudasai
doctor	isha (or) sensei
chemist	kusuriya
medicine	kusuri
hospital	byooin
ambulance	kyukyusha
body	karada
eye	me
ear	mimi
nose	hana
mouth	kuchi
arm	ude
leg	ashi

GENERAL

telephone	denwa
international telephone	kokusai denwa (dial 0051)
Just a moment	Chotto matte
hey!	ano ne!
no smoking car	kinnen sha
fast/slow	haiyai/yukuri
hot/cold	atsui/samui
near/far	chikai/toi
big/small	okii/chisai
long/short	nagai/michikai
narrow/wide	semai/hiroi
love/hate	ai/kirai
cheap/expensive	yasui/takai
beautiful	kirei

wonderful	subarashi
great!	sugoi
full/empty	ipai/suite imasu
drunk	yopparai
happy/sad	shiawase/sabishi
healthy	genki (also used as a greeting among friends: 'Genki?-Genki yo!')
good/bad	ii/dame
delicious/tasteless	oishi/mazui
sleep	nemuri
I want to sleep	Nemutai
shop (store)	mise
museum	hakubutsukan
bookshop	hon ya san
restaurant	shokudo

DIRECTIONS

up	ue ('oo-e')
down	shita
right	migi
left	hidari
in front of	mae ri
behind	ushiro ni
north	kita
south	minami
west	nishi
east	higashi
stairs	kaidan
lift	erebeta

JAPANESE FOOD

Entering a restaurant for the first time, the greatest hurdle, even after years in the country, is that the menu is unreadable. In some places, you can drag the waitress outside and point to the plastic mock-up of your selection in the window on the street.

It helps to learn various cuisines and how to recognise the types of restaurants that serve them. Nearly all restaurants in Japan are speciality shops and tend to have a particular 'look' about them. They will serve sushi, or tempura, or Chinese food (liberally interpreted), or teppan yaki; seldom will you encounter a place that serves all of them. Finding out what you like takes time and nerve. Time, because there are so many kinds of shops; and nerve, because it means trying things new, unusual, and yes, sometimes awful. Go around peering in doors that may look like you have no business opening them. Don't be intimidated by the owners' and customers' reactions to you, a foreigner, when you stick your head in the door. It may have been quite some time (if ever) since the last Gaijin stepped in. Usually, the reticent reception at your appearance stems from the owner's fear of serving you poorly, thus embarrassing both of you.

When you enter a place for the first time you have to feel it out quickly. In Tokyo they may not bat an eyelid at your appearance, while at a little neighbourhood sushi bar in Niigata they may go positively glacial. Nearly anywhere, you can assuage their fears by smiling, doing a light, informal bow and perhaps uttering an appropriate greeting for the time of day.

Besides the great variety of Japanese food there are many 'foreign' food places. Great Indian food, good Italian, French, Vietnamese, Malay and many other kinds are to be found in the larger cities. Don't hesitate to try these places; often their owners are so fanatically dedicated to the type of food they serve that the quality is excellent. Subject to regional variation, the basic types of Japanese food are:

Sushi: You may have tried this raw fish, seaweed and rice delicacy at home, but even if you didn't like it there, give it another try in Japan where its preparation is a high art. The best sushi is made with fish just hours old, relatively easy in this island nation. You'll find it is a varied and delightful cuisine. Try some down in the Tsukiji fish market, or on the wharf in Yobuko Town, Kyushu. You might want to avoid it as fast food on trains, etc., where you're unsure about its age, because it can be chewy and generally unappetising.

Sashimi: This is it: raw fish. Raw, but not unprepared. More effort goes into the slicing, arrangement and preparation of raw goodies than if the same item were cooked. You will be served sashimi for dinner in all ryokan and minshuku, so it's a good idea to learn to like it. Try adding a little lemon juice if the texture is just too... slippery. Add enough lemon juice and it will seem just like cooked fish. The Japanese will slice up anything out of the water and eat it, including the poisonous Fugu fish. Years of schooling are required before one can serve this fish without causing neurological disorders or fatalities. All other fish and shellfish you'll be served will be safe.

Soba: Noodles. Soba is a slender buckwheat noodle, while its fatter cousin 'udon' is made of white flour. Both are served in a delightful broth, just a few degrees the low side of boiling. Add vegetables, tempura shrimp and watercress, a bit of 'karashi' (chili pepper) and you have an inexpensive treat that is very sustaining. The Chinese noodle 'ramen' is a slender noodle often fried and mixed with meat and vegetables — very tasty. Noodles, particularly soba, are the staple foods of the traveller because they are served in stations throughout the land.

Teppan Yaki: Benihana food — meats, fish and vegetables cooked on hot steel. When you just have to have a steak, this is where you'll find a good one. Usually delicious, always expensive.

Yakitori: Chicken kebabs, pretty simple and very good. Available everywhere, these (cooked) titbits are popular with Gaijin and Japanese alike. Order some with sauce (tare) and some grilled with salt (shioyaki). The chef always has some new variations going. Look at what fellow diners order and don't be afraid to request the same by way of a little judicious pointing.

Okonomiyaki: Popular in the Kansai or Osaka area, this 'Japanese pizza' of flour, egg cabbage and various meats and usually some squid is grilled on teppan (steel) and covered with shaved dried fish and sosu. Sosu (sauce), on the tables in most smaller restaurants, is made of tomato ketchup and Worcestershire sauce. You will sometimes find it served on yatai late at night in Tokyo.

Yatai: Street carts, the salvation of late night drinkers and anyone who loves midnight snacks. These small carts appear after dark in towns across the land, serving everything from octopus balls (takoyaki) to roasted chestnuts and oden, a mixture of fish cakes, cabbage, tofu and whatever else is in stock tonight. The chestnut cart vendors roam the streets on winter nights with a plaintive wail of song and haunting pipe music.

Sukiyaki: Japanese stew, great in cold weather. Finely sliced, well marbled beef, onions, scallions, mushrooms, bamboo shoots and more in a broth of sake, soya and sugar. The ingredients are cooked as you eat and then dipped in whipped raw egg. The egg is optional but it makes the dish.

Tempura: Vegetables of all sorts as well as fish and/or shrimp dipped in a light, slightly crunchy batter, served absolutely sizzling hot. Outstanding tempura is hard to find, but even run-of-the-mill quality is quite edible.

Kaiseki ryori: The epitomy of Japanese cuisine to most people. Of extraordinary variety and delicacy, kaiseki ryori is designed to be eaten before the tea ceremony. Many small portions are served in a predetermined sequence. Good ryokan frequently serve a version of it for dinner. Kyoto Ryori is a variation you'll enjoy when you get to that city.

Inaka ryori: Country inn style food. A variety of foods cooked over charcoal and served with sauces and whatever the cook finds appropriate. Kushiyaki is a variation you'll find in the town of Niigata.

Kushikatsu: Pork and or chicken fried in a batter and served with mountains of cabbage and sosu. Cheap and good, it is often found in subterranean shopping centres/train stations.

Tonkatsu: Crispy breaded pork cutlet served with a scrumptious barbecue-like sosu and salad. I love it.

Teishoku: This type of meal can be a number of things such as tonkatsu or katsu (beef), served as a 'plate' with rice, soup and a salad. A good way to order lunch. Ask for 'Katsu teishoku kudasai'.

Seto: Workingman's lunch. Small restaurants in average neighbourhoods usually have a set lunch (ranchi seto), the special of the day. More food for less cash.

Vikingu: Viking as in smorgasbord or breakfast buffet. Served in most western-style hotels and business hotels, you can eat enough to get you through the day for a very reasonable price. The spread usually includes both western and Japanese foods. Take advantage of these when possible.

Kissaten: Coffee shops. These are everywhere and oh so nice when you need them. Foreigners always remark on the astronomical price of coffee in Japan. In these small, comfortable little shops you're paying for a place to sit down and get away from it all for a while. The coffee is expensive to pay the high rent. They have small libraries of newspapers and manga (comic books) to take the worker's mind off his cares while he rests. The coffee is usually fantastic.

McDonalds: We all know what these are. The Japanese love them. They can provide you a link to home when gastronomic culture shock strikes. Best of all, they almost always have toilets.

FOOD VOCABULARY
o-ohan rice specifically, food in general
nikku meat (usually beef)
bekon bacon
hamu ham
buta nikku pork
rosu roast beef (but not what you think — usually a tough fatty piece of meat fried and served as tonkatsu; in good places it's good.)
tori chicken (literally, bird)

o-sushi sushi
sakana fish
kani crab
ebi shrimp
oki ebi lobster
unagi eel
uni sea urchin
ikka squid
maguro tuna
hammachi yellow tail
kaki oysters
hamaguri clam

wasabi horseradish mustard
o-shoyu soy sauce
sosu Japanese sauce with ketchup and Worcestershire

yasai vegetables
gohan rice
tamanegi onion
kuri cucumber

retasu lettuce
kinoko mushroom (generic)
shitake a fine white mushroom
kabetsu cabbage
take no ko bamboo shoots
ninjin carrot
jagaimo potato
ninnikku garlic
remon lemon
meron melon (expensive)
ringo apple (can be very expensive; try Fuji ringos)
orenji orange
mikan Japanese orange (good)
ichigo strawberry

sato sugar
hachimitsu honey

pan bread
tamago eggs
bata butter
tosto toast
pinatsu bata peanut butter
jamu jam
mixto sando Japanese tea sandwiches
sandoichi sandwich
kare raisu curry rice

o-mizu water
sumetai mizu cold water
o-yu hot water
o-cha green tea, no caffeine
ban-cha tea made with roasted rice
ko-cha regular Chinese tea with caffeine
miruku milk
kurimu cream
jusu juice
beeru beer

o-sake liquor, especially rice wine
wainu wine (skip it)
mizu wari scotch and water, the national drink
sho chu rice liquor
shochu remon shochu cocktail, lemony
bancha wari a popular hot drink in Hokkaido made with bancha and shochu
masu zake cold sake in a cedar box
kora cola

MORE USEFUL INFORMATION

FESTIVALS

All Japan
January 1 Ganjitsu (New Year's Day)
January 2-6 Daruma Ichi, good luck dolls sold at temples
February 3 Setsubun (Bean-Throwing Festival) at many temples
March 3 Hinamatsuri (Doll Festival)
Spring Cherry Blossom Festival starts early April in the south, moves north through early May
May 5 Kodomo-No-Hi (Children's Day)
July 7 Tanabata (Star Festival)
July 13-16 O-Bon Festival (crowded everywhere!)
August National holiday season (crowded everywhere!)
Autumn Autumn colours start early October in Hokkaido, move south through November
November 15 Shichi-go-san (Children's visiting Day at shrines)
December 31 Joya-No-Kane (New Year's Eve)

Aomori
August 1-7 Nebuta Matsuri Festival

Fukuoka
May 3-4 Hakata Dontaku Festival, parade
July 15 Hakata Yamagasa Festival

Himeji
October 14-15 Kenka Matsuri Festival, Matsubara Shrine

Hiroshima
August 6 Peace Ceremony, Peace Memorial Park

Ise
April 5-8 Kagura-sai, Ise Shrines

Karatsu
November 2-4 Okunchi Festival, Karatsu Shrine

Kyoto
May 15 Aoi Matsuri (Hollyhock Festival), Shimogamo and Kamigamo Shrines
May, third Sunday Mifune Matsuri Festival, Oi River
July 16-17 Gion Matsuri, parade
August 16 Daimonji Bonfire, Mt Nyoigatake
October 22 Jidai Matsuri (Festival of Eras), Heian Shrine,

procession; Fire Festival, Yuki Shrine, Kurama
December 31 Okera Mairi Ceremony, Yasaka Shrine

Lake Akan, Hokkaido
October 8–10 Marimo Matsuri

Miyajima
Mid July Kangensai Music Festival, Itsukushima Shrine

Nara
January 5 Grass Fire Ceremony on Mt Wakakusayama
February 3 Lantern Festival, Kasuga Shrine
March 13 Kasuga Festival, Kasuga Shrine
December 17 On-Matsuri Festival, Kasuga Shrine, procession

Nikko
May 17–18 Grand Festival, Toshogu Shrine
April 16–17 Yayoi Matsuri, Futaarasan Shrine, procession
October 17 Autumn Festival, Toshogu Shrine

Morioka
June 15 Chagu-Chagu Umakko (Horse Festival)

Osaka
June 14 Rice-Planting Festival, Sumiyoshi Shrine

Sapporo
February 5–9 Snow Festival

Tokyo
January 6 Dezomeshika (New Year's Parade of Firemen)
Late April Festivals at Yasukuni and Meiji Shrines
May, third weekend Sanja Matsuri Festival, Asakusa Shrine
June 1–2 Hanashobu (Iris Exhibition), Meiji Shrine
June 10–16 Sanno Festival, Hie Shrine
Late September-Early October Grand Tokyo Festival, parades
October 11–13 Oeshiki Festival, Hommonji Temple
October 31-November 3 Autumn Festival, Meiji Shrine
Mid November Tori-no-ichi (Rake Fair), Otori Shrines
Mid December Hagoita-Ichi Fair (Year-End Market), Asakusa Kannon Temple

For a complete listing of trade fairs and shows throughout Japan, get a copy of *Exhibitions, Fairs & Events in Japan* from any Japan National Tourist Organisation office.

INFORMATION SOURCES

In the UK

Japan National Tourist Organisation is a good advance information source. Write to their London office and they'll keep your letter box full of brochures, pamphlets and newsletters. Call them to ask questions and get specific advice.

Tokyo: 2-10-1 Yuraku-cho, Chiyoda-ku, Tokyo 100, Japan. Tel: (03)-216-1902.
London: 167 Regent Street, London W1R 7FD. Tel: 01-734 9638.

The **Japan Travel Bureau** will also be able to help with advice and travel arrangements.
London: 190 Strand, London WC2R 1DT. Tel: 01-836 9367.

In Japan

Japan Travel-Phone, a free English-language information service for travellers in Japan, can help with language difficulties and give advice on good restaurants and accommodation. Until recently you had to go through a telephone operator (who often spoke no English) to call the Travel-Phone. Now you can dial direct (9:00-17:00 daily):
Eastern Japan: (0120)-222-800
Western Japan: (0120)-444-800
Tokyo JNTO: 502-1461
Kyoto JNTO: 371-5649

Japan Association of Travel Agents will handle complaints about services provided by its members. Contact them at Zen-Nittu Kasumigaseki Building, 3-3-3, Kasumigaseki, Chiyoda-ku, Tokyo 100, Japan. Tel: (03)-592-1271.

YOUTH HOSTELS

Youth hostels offer a low-price alternative accommodation to those travellers willing to sacrifice privacy and comfort in favour of budget. Accommodation is dormitory-style, and guests must provide their own sheets or rent them at an additional charge. The price at most Japanese youth hostels is 2,700 yen (£12.25) per night. The maximum stay is three consecutive nights. Reservations are strongly advised.

There is no maximum age limit; if you do not already have the required membership card from an IYH hostel in another country, you can get one for 3,000 yen (£13.50) at the Japan Youth Hostels national office, Hoken Kaikan, 1-1, Sadohara-cho, Ichigaya, Shinjuku-ku, Tokyo 162. They can also provide a complete list of hostels in Japan.

Youth hostels convenient to the tour route suggested in this book include:

Tokyo
Tokyo International Youth Hostel, 21-1 Kakuragashi, Shinjuku-ku, Tel: 235-1107.

Izu Peninsula (Shimoda)
Gensu Youth Hostel, Tel: 05586-2-0035, 25 minutes from Shimoda Eki by bus.

Ise Area
Youth Hostel Kontaiji, 3-24-1 Toba, Tel: (0599) 24-3035. Short walk from Toba Eki. Men only.

Kyoto
Higashiyama Youth Hostel, 112 Shirakawabashi-goken-cho, Sanjo-dori, Higashiyama-ku, Kyoto 605, Tel: 761-8135. 20 minutes from Kyoto Eki by bus.

Nara
Nara Youth Hostel, 1716 Horencho, Tel: 22-1334.

Kotohira
Youth Hostel Kotohira Seinen-No-Ie, 1241, Kawanishi-otsu, Kotohira-machi, Nakatado-gun, Kagawa-ken 766, Tel: (08777) 3-3836. Short walk from Kotohira Eki.

Hiroshima
Hiroshima Youth Hostel, 1-13-6, Ushita-shin-machi, Higashiku, Hiroshima City 730, Tel: (082) 221-5343. 10-minute bus ride from Hiroshima Eki.

Hatomizaki
None. See 'National Citizens' Hotel' information in Tour 13.

Sado Island
Hosen kan Youth Hostel, 1111 Katagami, Niibo-mura, Sadogun, Niigata Pref., Tel: 025942-3125.

Ura-Bandai
Ura-bandai Youth Hostel, Goshikinuma, Ura-bandai, Azumakyoku, Fukushima-ken 969-27, Tel: (024132) 2811.

Kanazawa
Kanazawa Youth Hostel, Tel: 0762-52-3414.

Nikko
Nikko Youth Hostel, 2854, Tokorono, Nikko City, Tel: 0288-54-1013.